Raising GODLY GIRLS

Deb Burma
with Courtney Burma

CONCORDIA PUBLISHING HOUSE • SAINT LOUIS

To the king and queen of my childhood palace - my parents,
Dick and Gene Hudson: your godly influence prepared me to raise royalty
of my own. Thank you for pointing me to Christ and modeling His grace.

To the many mothers who walked beside me during this writing journey:
you humbly shared your real-life stories and lessons learned while raising
godly girls. Thank you for your words, encouragement, and prayers.

To my faithful friend and editor, Peggy Kuethe: your gentle guidance
and professional counsel enabled this labor of love to become a reality.
Thank you for making my words sing!

Published by Concordia Publishing House
3558 S. Jefferson Avenue, St. Louis, MO 63118-3968
1-800-325-3040 · www.cph.org

Text © 2015 by Deb Burma

Manufactured in China

Library of Congress Cataloging-in-Publication Data

Burma, Deb.
  Raising godly girls / Deb Burma.
     pages cm
  Includes bibliographical references and index.
  ISBN 978-0-7586-4775-7 (alk. paper)
  1. Mothers and daughters--Religious aspects--Christianity. 2. Girls--Religious life. 3. Child rearing--Religious aspects--Christianity. 4. Parenting--Religious aspects--Christianity.
  I. Title.

  BV4529.18.B87 2015
  248.8'431--dc23
                                        2015015954

1 2 3 4 5 6 7 8 9 10   25 24 23 22 21 20 19 18 17 16 15

TABLE OF CONTENTS

Once Upon a Time

$\mathcal{O}$nce upon a time, a brand new baby girl was born. She was adored by her parents and was cradled in their care. To them, she was priceless, incredible, and beautiful. She was also precious in the sight of His Majesty (1 Samuel 26:24), who claimed her as His own beloved daughter and even made her an heir to His treasure and a princess of His kingdom (Romans 8:17). The remarkable thing about this baby girl was that, although she had earthly parents, His Majesty was her *heavenly* Father. In fact, He was her Creator. She was His own workmanship (Ephesians 2:10). His Majesty knitted her together in her mother's womb and proclaimed her to be wonderfully made (Psalm 139:13–14). Even before the world was created, He chose when and where and to whom this precious baby girl would be born (Ephesians 1:4). He formed all of her days for her, writing each day in His book before even one of them dawned (Psalm 139:16). And as she grew, she became more beautiful in the image of her heavenly Father (2 Corinthians 3:18), and she had a heart that was capable of much love because of the love He first gave her (1 John 4:19).

And so goes the beginning of your precious princess's life in *story* form, filled with truth and annotated with promises straight from Scripture. Your daughter has been created, chosen, and redeemed by her Savior. She is the apple of God's eye. She is the princess of a King. And her real-life story in Christ has oh-so-beautiful beginnings!

YOUR DAUGHTER'S REAL-LIFE STORY

We've read other stories that begin with "once upon a time" and tell of a princess's beauty, identity, value, and attributes. Beyond that, however, the similarities between these make-believe tales and your real-life daughter's story appear to end. But do they? While other once-upon-a-time stories are made up, the result of an author's creativity, your daughter's story is reality; it is not dreamed or imagined or written by the Brothers Grimm, C. S. Lewis, or Walt Disney. But her story does, indeed, have an author: God, the author of her life, has written every word on each page.

Many fairy tales include fanciful imagery such as palaces, carriages, and kingdoms and contain royal characters such as kings, queens, princes, and princesses. Similar imagery and characters fill the pages of your daughter's real-life story too, as I'll point out in the paragraphs and pages to follow. Occasionally, I'll draw upon truth or analogy found in fairy tales as they relate to her life in Christ.

As her mom, you want the fairy tale for your daughter, don't you? You want her life to be as perfect and as happy as any life can ever be. You promise to protect her from the dragons and wicked witches, from the snares and hardships that are so often part of life. Yet you know that real life is full of tribulation; Jesus Himself tells us that (John 16:33). You know that no one really lives the fairy tale. Today's news and cultural expectations are frightening because they are real threats, so you are motivated to try even harder to protect and to prepare your daughter. You love her, so you do your best to guide her footsteps through the dark and scary forest. You teach her to make wise choices and to be safe. You lead her to seek healthy relationships. You coach her to be responsible and well behaved. You train her according to God's Word. After all, that's your job—to raise her to be a godly girl from the moment of her conception to the moment of her final breath. That's the vocation the Lord God chose for you before the beginning of time. That's His plan for her as well.

Every story has conflict, someone or some situation that stands in the way of the protagonist's goal. Fairy-tale conflict usually comes in the form of a wicked character, supernatural force, or fantastical being. The conflict is resolved when the hero—Prince Charming, for instance—saves the day by rescuing the princess and giving her a happily-ever-after ending. You see where this is going, don't you? Your daughter's conflict comes in the form of the real world, the devil, and her own human nature. And her hero is, of course, her Lord and Savior, Jesus Christ, who defeated sin, death, and the devil for her! Jesus cut a clear path through the thorny, dark, and demon-filled world so He could take her to eternal life in heaven. And your princess will live happily ever after with Him there!

Although your daughter's story may not read exactly like a classic fairy tale, you can be assured that she *is royalty* and that her real-life story is far more engaging than any made-up tale, for the life God has prepared for her in Christ is better and more beautiful than anyone can ever imagine.

A CHILD OF GOD

As I seek to encourage you in this book, speaking to you from my heart, I'll refer to my daughter and yours singularly, although I realize you may be raising more than one godly girl. Each is a uniquely created princess with her own life story in Christ; each is a daughter of the heavenly Father, a child of God:

 See what kind of love the Father has given to us, that we should be called *children of God*; and so we are. 1 John 3:1 (emphasis added)

 You have received the Spirit of adoption as sons [and daughters], by whom we cry, "Abba! Father!" The Spirit Himself bears witness with our spirit that we are *children of God*. Romans 8:15–16 (emphasis added)

 Your princess is an adopted daughter of the **"King of kings and Lord of lords"** (1 Timothy 6:15): **He chose us in Him before the foundation of the world. . . . In love He predestined us for adoption as [children] through Jesus Christ, according to the purpose of His will.** Ephesians 1:4–5

PRINCESS

For centuries, in earthly kingdoms as well as in fairy tales, the title "princess" meant a daughter of the king and queen and possibly even an heir to the throne. A princess was royalty and was regarded for her virtue and character. Because of her station alone, she was reputed to be reverent, respectful, and obedient. Who wouldn't want that for her daughter? Initially, though, I hesitated to use the princess theme as a description of our daughters' identity. Not because it isn't true, but because of what modern American culture has done to the definition of princess. Perhaps it's because America hasn't been part of a monarchy for centuries, but our current culture takes "princess" out of the correct context and casually tosses it around as a mere word that appears on bumper stickers and T-shirts. Princess has become a party theme and a line of fashion accessories. The word has even become a description for an attitude of entitlement. But a real princess is not a word, an image, or an attitude. A real princess is an identity, a definition . . . a name.

For decades, animated princesses have caught the attention and the hearts of children and adults on the big screen. When Disney launched its Princess Collection retail line in the late 1990s, an enormous trend began that continues today. According to a 2006 *New York Times* article, "princess" is the fastest-growing product line the company has ever created. Other toy manufacturers and retailers have followed suit, meeting consumers' demands for all things "princess."

Take a look at your princess. She's dressed according to her day's activities, right? She probably isn't wearing a ball gown with a tulle-covered hoopskirt. No jewel-encrusted crown graces her head. No elbow-length white kid gloves encase her arms. Unless she is playing dress-up or getting ready for a formal high school dance—or she's employed to play a princess at a theme park—she is likely not dressed in a splendorous display that turns heads and evokes gasps. Nevertheless, your daughter is a princess, more truly than the costumed actress sporting a tiara and waving to the crowd in the Christmas parade. Clad in jeans or pajamas or soggy diaper, she is a PRINCESS, through and through. Princess is her name, based on who she is from the inside out: a daughter of His Majesty, the King of kings!

CHOSEN TO RAISE ROYALTY

The Lord God has chosen you at this time, in this chapter of *your* life story, and put you in the very place (palace!) where you have been given the special purpose of raising this precious princess. (That makes you and your husband the *queen* and *king* of your palace.) You are a part of God's master plan, and so is she (as is every prince and princess under your roof). You and your husband play a critical role in the formation of your daughter's character and traits. By God's grace, you influence her life, behaviors, and worldview more than any other people from her beginnings and throughout her early adulthood or longer.

God has gifted you with this girl, this little one who calls you Mom or Mama or Mommy. He chose her for you; He chose you for her! You, too, are God's workmanship. You were created, in part, for the task of nurturing, loving, and leading your daughter to be a godly girl. Like her, you are a daughter of the King of kings—a princess in your own right. And now, in the Lord's timing, you are raising royalty. She needs you. Even more important: she needs her heavenly Father, His Majesty. (So do you!) She'll look to you and you'll look to the Lord, and as you do, you are teaching her to do the same. To desire to raise royalty is to look to your heavenly King for everything: for His lead, His direction, and His will, for His provision, protection, and pardon, all along the way. As her life story unfolds day by day, you are there to impact her life for Christ, point her to Him, and model His grace for her, day by day. Just like a princess in any monarchy is raised to be royalty.

Even before my princess was born, as I nervously contemplated motherhood, the Lord was placing faithful people and godly moms in my life and was guiding me into His Word. He used both to grow me and prepare me for the arrival of our princess, Courtney, and our firstborn prince, her twin brother, Chris. (Another prince, Cameron, followed a few years later.) The Lord blessed me with the vocation of motherhood, choosing me to raise these little ones in the reverent awe and love of their Lord and Savior. I was terrified. And at the same time, I couldn't wait to begin. What an overwhelming task; what an incredible privilege! From the first moment that I held those tiny bundles in my arms, I knew that the most important thing I could share with them was also the most important thing I possess, by God's grace: faith in Jesus. Without delay, my husband and I brought our little princess and prince before the waters of Holy Baptism, where they were received into God's kingdom. The same faith that flowed into me at my Baptism was now theirs. And then began that humble privilege and awesome responsibility to raise our kids. To bring them up in the one true faith, continually point them to Christ, and teach them His ways.

Throughout this book, I'll share with you triumphant moments when God's continual work in my life and in my daughter's has been most evident. But I must admit to you that in each and every area of my calling as a mom, I have stumbled, fallen, and even wondered if I have what it takes to be a parent. I've learned to lean into God's strong arms of grace, and I pray that you are led to do the same.

As I relate memories, personal experiences, and lessons learned along with practical advice and suggestions, I pray that they will speak to you, that through the words of these pages, you'll be greatly encouraged and equipped in your God-given vocation. I pray that you will receive reassurance, guidance, and grace—not only in your role as a mom (a kingdom worker who's raising royalty), but also as a daughter of the King of kings in your own walk with your heavenly Father.

While every chapter of *Raising Godly Girls* contains anecdotes and Scripture, ideas and advice specific to the topic, each chapter has a few things in common. Look for the following sections near the close of each chapter:

Don't Conform, Be Transformed!— In the words of Paul, **"be transformed by the renewal of your mind, that by testing you may discern what is the will of God, what is good and acceptable and perfect"** (Romans 12:2). I apply this scriptural truth to each chapter's topic as encouragement to you to live counterculturally by teaching and modeling for your daughter how not to conform to the ways of this world.

A Word of Grace— Here, you'll receive a word of reassurance that your sins are forgiven by God in Christ, specifically as it pertains to each chapter topic. God knows that every aspect of parenting presents a challenge. He also knows that we will make mistakes along the way. Over and over, our heavenly Father gives us His grace. He picks us up and enables us to continue in this Kingdom work, this noblest of tasks.

Show and Tell— You may recall bringing something special to school to *tell* your classmates about it and why it mattered to you as you *showed* what it was. On a much greater scale, you now share a life of show-and-tell with your daughter. You have countless opportunities to *tell* her all about Jesus and why your faith walk matters more to you than anything else, while *showing* her how to live according to His Word. By God's grace, you can show and tell as you live intentionally through your example and your words. Every chapter includes a wealth of show-and-tell examples, although they are not labeled as such. And at the close of every chapter, I share specific questions and ideas to ponder as you read this book alone or beside your growing girl, or as you discuss it with other moms.

Chapter 1

Only by Grace—
Raising Royalty by the Grace of God

And God is able to make all grace abound to you, so that having all sufficiency in all things at all times, you may abound in every good work. 2 Corinthians 9:8

GOOD VERSUS EVIL

I loved reading to my daughter, Courtney. I read board books with simple words and familiar photographs, picture books with bright illustrations and rhyming text, and fairy tales with timeless moral lessons. We read Bible story books that introduced her to amazing bits of history and God's Word for His people throughout time. And we read chapter books: historical fiction, mystery, adventure, fantasy, and more. When she was very little, she would snuggle on my lap and I would wrap my arms around her. As her attention span (and her legs) grew, she'd pick up a pile of her favorite books and curl up next to me for some quality reading time. Through her facial expressions, giggles, and gasps, I could see that she, like her mom, loves a good story.

Most of us love a good story, one full of adventure, romance, and conflict, with a *good versus evil* plot—as long as good wins and the end is a happy one. Who wants to read the final chapter only to close the cover with a sour stomach because all was lost and evil triumphed? That isn't how classic storybooks go, fiction or nonfiction.

Real life is a series of true tales of good versus evil. Real world battles rage around us. Every time we read the headlines in the paper, peek on the Internet, or turn on the TV, we are bombarded with bad news. At any moment, there is war, strife, political tension. Perhaps it appears to you that the world is growing more dangerous. That there is more crime, more violence, more disease and disaster. The bad news lurks close to home too. Perhaps it seems that your daughter faces more threat of harm than you did at her age, certainly more than your mom ever did. From teaching your toddler to hold on to the handrail when she's learning to go down the stairs to warning your teen about predators on social media, you are constantly on guard for her and continuously teaching her to be alert to danger.

If external threats aren't enough, we all face inner conflict as well. We want to *be* good and *do* good for God and for others, and we want our daughters to be that way too. But we struggle. Our thoughts run rampant. Our bodies revolt. Our hearts break. Like the apostle Paul, each of us can readily say that **"I do not do the good I want, but the evil I do not want is what I keep on doing"** (Romans 7:19). And like the psalmist, we cry, **"There is none who does good, not even one"** (14:3).

It's important for us to always remember that Satan, our very real enemy, is absolutely evil and wants our complete and total destruction. He will stop at nothing to take us down. Conversely, the Lord is the very definition of absolute and ultimate good, and He desires that all sinners would be saved from our sins, victorious over the evil with which we struggle, and delivered from it forever. **"Who will deliver me?"** continues Paul in Romans 7:24. It is only by the gift of God's grace that we are saved through faith (see Ephesians 2:8). And by His grace we can proclaim with Paul: **"Thanks be to God through Jesus Christ our Lord!"** (Romans 7:25). Jesus is our hero!

OUR HERO!

Although your daughter's life story will include her adventures, she is certainly not the hero of her own story (and neither are you or her dad). Incomparably greater than a dashing fairy-tale prince or a knight in shining armor who slays dragons in the land of make-believe, the hero of her real-life saga is Christ Jesus! He may not always be mentioned by name, but He appears on every page. He will always be with her, guiding, giving direction, and saving her. He always knows what she needs and is all-powerful to provide it. And what she will need—what we all need—more than anything throughout her life story is *rescue.*

Her hero willingly left the wonders of heaven where He was seated beside the King and enthroned in majesty and descended to this fallen world on a rescue mission of grace. True God and true man, Jesus fought victoriously and defeated the evil nemesis, death, and sin in one fell swoop. When Jesus died on the cross, He proved to Satan and all the world that He is our ultimate hero. His sacrificial death and His resurrection three days later are the perfect conclusion. A storybook hero may save the day for the storybook princess, but Christ did incomparably more—He saved your daughter's *life!* Only a true hero would sacrifice Himself to save the life of the ones He loves. Jesus said, **"The thief comes only to steal and kill and destroy. I came that they may have life and have it abundantly"** (John 10:10).

THIS I KNOW

My little prince and princess and I had just completed another adventurous grocery-shopping expedition. (If you've ever taken two-and-a-half-year-old twins to the grocery store, then you know what kind of adventure we had.) While they had been having fun, I'd been flustered and impatient as I tried to juggle kids, grocery lists, coupons, and car keys, while failing to remember what it was that I had forgotten. (Again, if you've been there, then you know what I mean.) I plopped down into the driver's seat of our royal carriage (our minivan), collected myself, and peered in the rearview mirror. The twins were strapped in their car seats, contentedly chattering to each other about their favorite weekly outing and sharing in toddler language the exciting things they had seen in the ice cream aisle. All was well. So I backed out of the parking space and took off for home. Still frustrated and distracted by my thoughts, I welcomed the opportunity to just *be still* during our ride time.

Then, when we were almost home, I froze. Something was definitely missing. Purse—check. Keys—check (of course; I was driving). Kids—double check. Groceries—OH NO! I had taken advantage of the wonderful perfect-for-moms drive-up service that our grocery store offered, but I had failed to drive up! My thoughts whirled: *What if someone else had taken my groceries? What if everything was melted or spoiled in the warm Texas weather? What if they had put everything back and I had to do it all over again?*

I was fretting out loud as I turned the van around, noticeably shaken by my absentminded error, when Courtney shouted out words I will never forget:

"It's gonna be okay, Mommy! Jesus still loves you!"

Out of the mouths of babes! Instantly, a wave of warmth and calm swept over me, washing away my flustered thoughts. I was flooded by the truth of this little one's sweet words. Jesus STILL loves me. No matter what. Even when I forget my groceries, lose my patience, and allow little things to frustrate and upset me. This beautiful truth is mine all the time. Jesus' love for me is so great that He comes to me, like a knight in shining armor, in the midst of my mess-ups and showers His grace and forgiveness upon me. Yes, even on my most absent-minded-flustered-mom distracted days.

I admit that forgetting the groceries isn't such a big thing in the larger context of what can go wrong. I know many women who face greater frustrations, greater inconveniences than my short return trip to the grocery store. But I don't know of a better way to regain the right perspective. This reminder of a simple yet profound truth led me to want to pull over right then, jump out of the royal carriage, lift my hands toward heaven, and shout, "Thank You, God!" In addition to THAT, the fact that these most reassuring words came from a child just two-and-a-half years old touched my heart deeply. Her proclamation revealed that she was listening, learning, and grasping the Gospel truth of God's love in Christ.

Courtney had heard these words many times already. She had heard them repeatedly in church, during Sunday School class, and at home from her father and me. She and her brother had already learned to sing "Jesus loves me, this I know, for the Bible tells me so!" And because she had faith from the moment of her Baptism, she was able to share what she knew already—that Jesus still loved me. In the moment of her mother's panic, these words were the *first* to come to her little heart and mind, the first to tumble out of her mouth, praise the Lord. They were the most comforting words I could hope to hear.

So, Mommy, no matter what mess-ups, failures, or frustrations (large or small) come your way and threaten to ruin your day, no matter how many ways the evil nemesis tries to get a foothold as you parent your precious princess, remember that "It's gonna be okay, Mommy!" Jesus, your Savior, loves you in spite of your failures and in the midst of every detail of life. Nothing can separate you from His love. **"Nor height nor depth, nor anything else in all creation, will be able to separate us from the love of God in Christ Jesus our Lord"** (Romans 8:39).

By the way, I successfully retrieved those groceries. They weren't even spoiled!

BECAUSE YOU ARE HIS

I remember so well the days my children were born. Even before I first laid eyes on them, I had fallen head over heels in love with them. They had done nothing to deserve my love, but there I was, smitten by these little bundles merely because they were mine. My love for my children, though imperfect because of my sin, gives me a tiny little glimpse into the perfect love of my heavenly Father. He is head over heels in love with you and me and our little (or not-so-little) princesses! Not because of anything any of us has done; not because we deserve His love. But He loves us simply because we are His. He made us. We are His precious daughters— His children. **"Beloved, we are God's children now"** (1 John 3:2).

As you raise your daughter, you know that she is going to mess up. Some days more than others. You'll cringe at her mistakes and hurt with her in her pain. But you'll never stop loving her, no matter what, will you? Can you begin to picture what our Lord's limitless love looks like?

As a pleaser, I have often committed the error of relating performance with love, subconsciously placing one as a condition in connection with the other. As I was growing up, my parents gave me no reason to believe I would cease to be loved or would be loved any less if I failed to please them, neglected to perform a certain way, or massively messed up. Their love for me was not based on my performance but on who I was and still am: their daughter, their princess. Again, I must consider this truth in light of the perfect, limitless love of the Lord, which is far greater than that of even the most adoring parent. His love does not vary according to my actions, and what a relief that is, because my actions always fall short of His perfection. I'm reminded that nothing can separate me from His love! He loves me simply because I am His chosen and forgiven child in Christ. And nothing can keep me from loving my daughter; nothing can sever the special bond between us. It's a love that would lead me to do anything for my sweet princess. It's a love that (though imperfect) reflects the perfect love of the Father toward us and toward our daughters. In fact, our love for them flows out of His love for us. **"We love because He first loved us"** (1 John 4:19). His love enables us to continually grow in love for others: **"May the Lord make you increase and abound in love for one another"** (1 Thessalonians 3:12). It's a love that would lead Him to do anything for us. And He has, in the greatest act of love ever known. As you read this beloved nugget of truth from John 3:16, please insert your name: "For God so loved _____, that He gave His only Son, that _____, [who] believes in Him should not perish but have eternal life."

SUFFICIENT!

The difficult days of parenting may lead you to feelings of dismay. When you make mistakes and you feel like a failure, you may question your abilities and doubt your competency in the not-for-the-faint-of-heart vocation called mother-hood. The truth is, you're not competent on your own. Even someone like the apostle Paul himself recognized his incompetency. When he wrote to the Corinthians about the task of sharing the Gospel he and his fellow apostles had been given, he admitted, **"Not that we are sufficient in ourselves to claim anything as coming from us, but our sufficiency is from God"** (2 Corinthians 3:5). So do not be dismayed! Out of God's inseparable love for you in Christ, and by the Spirit's power at work in you, He is equipping you with everything you need for this great adventure. After all, He put you into this adventure in the first place. He is your Creator and your daughter's Creator. He is in control. So lean into Him for strength and look to Him for wisdom, guidance, patience, perseverance, and more. (You'll continually need these in abundance.) **"And God is able to make all grace abound to**

you, so that having all sufficiency in all things at all times, you may abound in every good work" (2 Corinthians 9:8). In Christ, you are completely sufficient for this special task He's given you, and yes, you will abound, by His grace, in this "good work" of raising royalty.

GRACE FURTHER DEFINED

Have you ever stood under a rushing waterfall? If not, can you imagine it? It engulfs you fully, takes away your breath. That is how God showers His grace upon you. **"In [Christ] we have . . . the forgiveness of our trespasses, according to the riches of His grace, which He lavished upon us"** (Ephesians 1:7–8). And this is the message of grace—a message of utmost importance—that I am compelled to share with you here in chapter 1. I pray that you will grasp the grace that God gives to you, as you continue to read. God's rich grace—His unmerited favor—provides pardon for our sins. We don't deserve His grace, but He lavishes it upon us anyway! In fact, it overflows: **"The grace of our Lord overflowed for me with the faith and love that are in Christ Jesus"** (1 Timothy 1:14). By this *free gift* of grace, we receive forgiveness no matter where we have been or what we have done. God gives us victory over sin and eternal death because of His Son, Jesus, who died for us on the cross. Envision standing under His steady stream of grace and allowing it to completely cover you. In the overflow, you are free to share the same undeserved grace and forgiveness with your daughter, with those around you, and with the rest of the world. They are covered by His grace through you because you are a messenger of the Father's forgiveness, by the power of the Holy Spirit working in and through you.

WE LIVE FORGIVEN *AND* FORGIVING!

God's grace covers us even when we've failed *again* and when our daughter has disobeyed *again*. On those most difficult days—when she has messed up, tried your patience, misbehaved, disobeyed, failed to listen to your godly guidance, and more—take a deep breath and pray. And as you consider an appropriate response or necessary discipline, remember that God's grace is freely given *to* and shared *through* you. (If necessary, reread this page when you find yourself in the middle of those difficult days!) The Lord will enable you to continue raising up your godly girl in loving discipline, effectively separating the child from the choice, all out of love. Because grace is given to you, you can extend the same as you say, "I don't like your choice, but I love you. Nothing can separate you from my love. I forgive you."

This works in the opposite direction as well. It's because I live forgiven by the Lord that I know just how much I need to seek the forgiveness of my daughter. As humbling as it was for me to go before my little girl for the first time and admit that I messed up, that I overreacted, that I was wrong, the Lord did something amazing with the words "I'm sorry." He redeemed the moment.

God uses our humble confessions for our good, for our girls' good, and for His purposes. First, with God's help, we recognize when we've messed up and we're remorseful. When we admit our sins, we teach our princesses that we all make mistakes and we all need forgiveness. Second, we model the truth that we are forgiven by the Lord and actively seek the same forgiveness from others. Third, we are teaching her to appropriately respond with an honest "I forgive you" and not a nonchalant or even insincere "That's okay." Because it's not okay. Our sins against God and against one another are *not* okay.

Sin separates us from God. Sin can damage or even destroy relationships. Unforgiven sin can destroy our relationship with our Lord. But as we come before Him, sorry for our sins, He says, "I forgive you." The Bible reminds us in 1 John 1:9, **"If we confess our sins, He is faithful and just to forgive us our sins."** God forgives us because that's what He does. Jesus is our Savior from sin; therefore, we are forgiven. And forgiven, we can freely forgive! We are told in Colossians 3:13 to **"forgiv[e] each other; as the Lord has forgiven you, so you also must forgive."** When we forgive as we have been forgiven, then God's rich, lavish grace flows out of us and onto others!

There's an important place for apology in every relationship. What does your daughter overhear you saying to your husband when you recognize your fault in an argument? What does she witness when you interact with her siblings or extended family over difficult issues? Can she tell if you're holding a grudge, nursing bitterness, or failing to forgive someone? In each and every interaction, as you seek God's guidance and ask for a humble and repentant heart, you have the opportunity to shine Christ's light of forgiveness upon another, and the reflective glow of this extended grace is caught, remembered, and emulated by your precious princess.

DON'T CONFORM—BE TRANSFORMED!

"Do not be conformed to this world, but be transformed

by the renewal of your mind, that by testing you may discern what is the will of God, what is good and acceptable and perfect" (Romans 12:2). It's only by God's grace that we are able to effectively guide our daughters to lead a godly life, but the world tells us something else. If we conform to its ways, then we fall prey to the notion that parenting struggles mean we simply aren't trying hard enough. If our child succeeds, the world tells us that her success is somehow solely our achievement. The truth is, we will face our share of both struggles and successes while "training up" our daughters in the way they should go. And yes, because we are influential in their lives, we have an impact that contributes in both bad and good ways. But when we keep our focus on God's will and encourage our daughters to do the same, we can resist conformity to the world's child-raising directions and trust that God works in our lives and in the lives of our daughters to gently draw us closer to Him in every circumstance. (We'll talk about this more in chapter 8, *Growing Pains*.) As godly moms, we seek God's strength through the struggles, we rejoice in Him through our successes, and we thank Him for what we have experienced and how we have grown through <u>both</u>.

With growth comes transformation and discernment. As moms who desire nothing more than to see our dear daughters walking with the Lord, we rest in His grace, trusting that He works through every situation to make us and her more like Christ, to discern and desire to follow His "good and acceptable and perfect" will.

As you recall your kingdom-building adventures, do not focus on the things you haven't done well or on what you've seen other families do. Avoid comparing your life with what "everyone" in today's world appears to be doing. Yes, I know. This is cliché advice, but the urge to compare ourselves to others is difficult to resist. Case in point: When Courtney was young, it appeared to me that all the good moms were playing dolls and having tea parties with their little girls, but I didn't do that. I loved to bake with her, read to her, and spend time together in other ways, but I wasn't very patient when it came to playing together. *Did I need to make excuses as to why I didn't play with my princess?* And another example: Our humble palace was straight out of the middle ages because it didn't contain the latest video game console. Accusations came at me from a number of directions, and I felt guilty. *Would my children be the social outcasts of the community? Did I need to hide the fact that I didn't engage them in the latest electronic games?* (Oh sure, we had computer learning games, but I was informed that they were NOT the same thing!) While these examples may sound small or materialistic, these cultural expectations and others like them led me to believe that I was *insufficient* as a parent.

Maybe you have also felt that you've fallen short, especially when you observe that other moms conform to the latest cultural craze. Do not worry about the ways other moms and daughters interact or about how the world attempts to dictate what you must have or do or be. If all the "good" moms you know jumped off the Empire State Building, would you do the same? Of course not! Remind yourself that if you choose to limit your daughter's activities and she doesn't get to take tap lessons or if you don't take her to the latest pop star's concert (or to the tattoo parlor or whatever "everyone else" is doing for their daughter), you are still providing her with the care and nurture that God has called you to give. Ask for God's strength to focus instead on what is unique to you and your family. Trust that the Lord is leading you in the path He has set before you. And one day soon, your daughter will remember something significant and special that you may have overlooked. (Just recently, Courtney was reminiscing about at-home playtime while growing up. She volunteered, "We didn't have video games, so we had more time to play and create. You provided us with craft supplies, toys, ideas, cardboard play structures, and costumes. You did things with us, but also let us learn on our own; it was a nice balance. You gave us opportunities to do constructive things, and then you let us 'have at it'!" And to think that I had lamented for years that these were just a few of the ways in which I failed to conform or become a "good" mom.)

A WORD OF GRACE

Ask your heavenly Father for a fresh supply of grace for every moment and each new day. Stop beating yourself up over the things you wish you had done differently. The only reason to recall the regrets of the past is to learn from them, ask for God's strength to resist them, and move forward in a new direction. God never intended you to go it alone, to parent in your own strength, somehow mustering up what you need on a case-by-case basis. Your heavenly Father reaches down to you daily with guidance and grace. Use God's Word as your compass as you teach your princess right from wrong, and help her discern good from evil. And, both of you, rest in His grace-filled Word, confident that His grace is sufficient.

SHOW AND TELL

1. Take a look at your precious girl, and consider the love you have for her. Now, take a moment to envision your Lord's limitless love for you AND her. You are both His priceless possessions—His children. Recall Christ's rescue as He scooped you up out of your sin and saved your life by His sacrificial death on the cross; He did the same for your dear daughter. Rejoice with her, and together, lift your hands to heaven and shout, "Thank You, God!" Today and every day, as you rely on God's grace to raise your princess, you can rest in the blessing of this gift that's yours in Christ Jesus.

2. How do you typically respond when you fail? Is your home a safe haven of grace and understanding? a place of recovery following your failure? God can use your times of failure to grow and transform you. You can learn from them. In the safe space of your palace, you get to practice seeking, receiving, and sharing grace and forgiveness. It's at home that you learn to live in humility and learn that it's by Christ's strength that you can get back up and try again. Think of a recent failure and recovery. What did you learn, and how have you grown as a result?

3. *Now, consider these questions and reflections as they apply to your daughter:* How do you typically respond when she fails? Is your home a safe haven of grace and understanding? a place of recovery following her failure? God uses her times of failure to grow and transform her. She can learn from them. In the safe space of your palace, she gets to practice seeking, receiving, and sharing

grace and forgiveness. She learns to live in humility and learns to understand that it is by Christ's strength that she can get back up and try again. Think of a recent failure. What do you think she has learned, and how has she grown as a result? Share and discuss with her.

4. Does your daughter witness you extending the gift of grace to others even when they don't deserve it? How have you modeled a life of grace to her lately? With God's help, what would you like to do differently?

Chapter 2

Fearfully and Wonderfully Made—
A Princess's True Identity

For You formed my inward parts; You knitted me together in my
mother's womb. I praise You, for I am fearfully and wonderfully
made. Psalm 139:13–14a

KNIT TOGETHER

It was love at first sight, wasn't it? The first
glimpse of her heartbeat or the initial peek at her tiny
fingers and toes, as displayed before you on the ultra-
sound screen. Or maybe it was your first look into her
precious face following the incredible news that you'd
received a child to adopt as your very own. Perhaps,
instead, it was the first time you smiled upon the
special girl who would later become your stepdaugh-
ter. Before that first look or that first tender touch,
the identity of this little one had already been given to
her. She is so much more than her current appearance
or the sum of her future accomplishments, and even
more than her place in your family and who she will be
in relation to her peers and those in authority over her.
She is a child of God, a chosen princess of the King.

Circle back to the beautiful beginnings of your daughter's life story in the opening words of this book. She has been "fearfully and wonderfully made." From her conception, God was busily forming every inward part, knitting her together, beautifully and artistically designing her—body and soul. The following verse from Psalm 139 goes on to say, **"My frame was not hidden from you, when I was being made in secret, intricately woven."** Even before you laid your eyes upon your daughter, her Creator saw her as He formed her and wove together every detail. He knew everything about her. He knew the color of her skin, her eyes, and her hair. He knew the sound of her laughter and her cries. He knew every intricate detail of her personality and her unique gifts and abilities. And He established her as part of your family.

THE ROOT OF HER TRUE IDENTITY

Maybe you're reading this thinking, *Yes, this is precious and true. But what does this have to do with raising royalty?* Whether your girl is two months, two years, or two decades old, remember the truth that her identity (and, for that matter, yours too) is rooted in her Savior, the Prince of Peace, who reconciled her with her Creator. She was bought at the ultimate price (1 Corinthians 7:23) of His own blood shed on the cross for her (1 Peter 1:18–19). She was chosen and adopted as God's own daughter in her Baptism. He says, **"I will be a father to you, and you shall be sons and daughters to Me"** (2 Corinthians 6:18).

Your daughter's identity is rooted in Christ and flows forward throughout her life story. If someone asked you to further define who she is, you would point to yourself and her father to proudly proclaim, "She's our daughter, of course!" She is a granddaughter, niece, sister, friend, and more. Yes, she is defined partially by her relationships, those that impact her by their influence upon her and in their interactions with her. We think of ourselves in the context of our relationships— you are your mother's daughter, your husband's wife. Identity defined this way is even more pronounced in an adolescent or teenager's life—she is that person's friend or part of a specific social group. When a friendship ends or a loved one moves away or passes away, relationships change. The loss of a relationship leaves all of us temporarily feeling a hole in our lives, doesn't it? Who are we, now that this person isn't in our life? That's why it's especially important that your princess learns and remembers that her earthly relationships alone cannot define who she is. First and foremost, she is a child of God in Christ.

GOD-GIVEN GIFTS

If your daughter was asked to further define herself, how might she reply? (Of course, this depends on whether she is two or twenty-two or somewhere between.) She might think first of her family and her identity in relationship to them, as we just discussed. She might describe her appearance. (Another topic that receives its own chapter.) She might also think to define herself in terms of her abilities, as my daughter did when she shared what she could do well: "I play the piano." When Courtney showed an aptitude for music at a young age, we sought direction that would enable this God-given gift to grow and blossom. And it did! Through piano lessons, Courtney recognized an area of giftedness where she could excel, with practice and patience. Years later, she would tell us that playing the piano gave her satisfaction because she recognized it as a gift from God that she was able to continually develop. It was a healthy outlet for stress long before she could define this as another benefit, and it even established in her a good work ethic (following many tearful times of arduous practice). Eventually, it became an area where she could serve others by using this specific gift.

Maybe you're just beginning to recognize gifts and talents in your very young girl. Help her, as she grows, to identify and seek out ways to begin developing and using those gifts. Or maybe you're already trying to keep up with the many ways your growing girl is striving to build upon, fine-tune, and thrive in her unique abilities. They are a special part of who she is and how she is wired for service to her Savior and to others. **"For we are His workmanship, created in Christ Jesus for good works, which God prepared beforehand, that we should walk in them"** (Ephesians 2:10). Isn't it exciting to think that God planned exactly how He would gift His child as He created her and bestowed upon her physical, intellectual, and spiritual gifts? You can help her, encourage her, and walk beside her as she "walk[s] in them." And as you do, be intentional about giving God the glory for every gift. When you glorify Him, you're seizing one of countless opportunities that you'll have to help her look to Him in every aspect of life. She needs ongoing reminders that **"every good gift and every perfect gift is from above"** (James 1:17). Her talents and abilities, as gifts from God, help define who she is—a unique child of His creation and choosing. Even if the world should dismiss some of these gifts or fail to notice them at all, that doesn't make them any less valuable or noteworthy, especially in the safe growing space of your home. And you have the joy and privilege of building her up in them. Maybe she's a good hugger, a helpful worker, or a patient listener. Maybe her gifts lie in academics, music, or athletics. Maybe she shows interest in communications, leadership, people-care, or technology.

Maybe she doesn't think she's anything special because someone or something has attempted to determine her identity for her and it has left her lacking. Gently remind your uniquely knitted child that she is indeed *fearfully and wonderfully made,* not to be compared to others or against their appearance, gifts, or accomplishments, but beautifully able to glorify God just as He made her to be: filled with unique purpose!

GOD'S GIFTS OF GRACE

Romans 12 provides us with a reminder of the vast variety of spiritual gifts God gives generously to His children. In a beautiful illustration, the apostle Paul compares each member of the Body of Christ to each part of the human body. Every Christian is given unique gifts for a special purpose, just as each part of our body is unique in purpose and function. All parts are needed, have a necessary function, and work together (see Romans 12:4–5). Explore these gifts with your daughter and help her to see why she shouldn't compare herself to anyone else. Even within your immediate family, her gifts have a unique and necessary place. Is she the hands or feet of your family? Does your daughter enjoy teaching or helping serve wherever she can? Is she an encourager or a generous giver? Does she possess leadership potential or the desire to help those who cannot help themselves? Guide your princess to prayerfully consider where her growing gifts of grace lie so she may use them well. **"Having gifts that differ according to the grace given to us, let us use them: if prophecy, in proportion to our faith; if service, in our serving; the** one who teaches, in his teaching; the one who exhorts, in his exhortation; the one who contributes, in generosity; the one who leads, with zeal; the one who does acts of mercy, with cheerfulness" (Romans 12:6–8).

Conversely, God created others with gifts she may not possess. *How exciting!* When given the opportunity to work together, our gifts complement one another's—to everyone's benefit and for God's glory.

As your daughter grows and recognizes more of her God-given gifts, and as she begins to use them and grow in them, ask God to provide specific opportunities for her to use them in church, at home, around the neighborhood, at school, in places of special need . . . maybe even around the world. Encourage her to use every spiritual blessing she has in Christ to her greatest potential. And meanwhile, prayerfully explore, grow in, and continue to use your own. Maybe you share some of the same gifts, or maybe your differing gifts can complement each other's and you can grow side by side. Together, take your chocolate chip cookies and help serve at a community event. Dramatize a Bible story dialogue during Sunday School or Vacation Bible School. Share your crafty creations with the residents of an assisted living center. Take your favorite book to library story time and read it aloud to the children. Lead a Bible study together at a mother-daughter retreat.

However you use your time, teach your daughter and show her by your example how she can benefit others and be a blessing to them by using the spiritual gifts, talents, and time with which God has gifted her.

The God-given combined gifts of personality, abilities, and talents will be used beautifully for her future vocations and for the opportunities He has in store to fulfill His purposes in her life. He is preparing her and working in her now (see Philippians 2:13), that she may be for someone the hands and feet of Christ in the years to come. She'll serve Him by serving someone who will be blessed by her abilities.

A GIFT SHARED

Although I had already seen many fruits of the years of labor that Courtney had put into piano practice, I was especially moved to see the impact upon another life as she shared her gift of music during a recital performance following her senior year of high school. Courtney's piano instructor, Carolee, had chosen an assisted-living facility as the location for the recital as a way to bless these residents, as well as the students' family members, with the gift of music. Several residents were wheeled in, and one gentleman in particular caught my eye. He appeared incoherent, and I wondered why he had been brought since he was unresponsive throughout most of the performance. As the oldest student, Courtney was chosen to play her final piece—a duet with Carolee—at the end of the recital. The piece they chose was an eloquent, stirring arrangement of "Jesus Loves Me." When they arrived at the recognizable chorus of the song, the formerly unresponsive gentleman lifted his head and belted out the words, "Yes, Jesus loves me! Yes, Jesus loves me! Yes, Jesus loves me! The Bible tells me so." I heard soft gasps around me as all eyes (not a dry one in the place!) turned to watch him. The words of this song, so deeply rooted in an old man's failing memory, came pouring out when the gift of music was shared in his presence that day. And the joy in his aged face was impossible to miss. The entire crowd was blessed through his response and the song itself. And Courtney saw the beauty of the gift she shared for the benefit of others and to the glory of God.

Expect God to open doors of opportunity as your princess continues to grow and to do things as only she can, according to her unique God-given design and for the people He places in her life story. As you instill in her, by your encouragement and your example, the desire to serve, give, and *do* whatever she does to the best of her ability, you're helping to establish a strong work ethic in her, even as she is exploring and learning more about her identity in Christ. From the Word, you can tell her, **"Whatever you do, work heartily, as for the Lord and not for men . . . you are serving the Lord Christ"** (Colossians 3:23–24). What a humble privilege to serve our Lord as we serve His children.

A word of caution: be careful not to allow your daughter to think that her gifts and abilities by themselves are what defines or identifies her. When we describe her repeatedly by her activities and accomplishments, appearance, or relationships, even if we're not verbalizing *"this* is who you are," we risk setting her up for a roller-coaster ride of feelings about her self-worth with the potential for derailment. What if she loses a particular skill? What if a talent gets her only so far in life and no farther? Is she no longer valued as a person? When your godly girl is firmly rooted and grounded in the fact that, no matter what, she is chosen by God in Christ, valued and cherished by Him, created uniquely for a purpose and loved eternally, then when external things change—when relationships end, when she doesn't think she's pretty, when report cards disappoint, when abilities seem lackluster next to others'—she can remember the beautiful beginnings of her life story in Christ (like the one you read at the beginning of this book) and proclaim, "I am fearfully and wonderfully made, a beloved and beautiful daughter of the King of kings!"

IF THE GLASS SLIPPER FITS . . .

Having defined your daughter's identity as a precious princess in her real-life story, a chosen and adopted child of the King, I'd like to share a further word picture with you. Indulge me as you open your memory or your storybook to the classic tale of Cinderella. Perhaps the following illustration will provide a fun and relevant visual for you as you talk to your princess (whatever her age) about her true identity.

You remember Prince Charming, of course. He had his palace officials search his father's kingdom high and low to find the mystery maiden with whom he had fallen in love at the grand ball. The glass slipper she had left behind was the only clue to her true identity. When the officials visited Cinderella's home and insisted that she try on the shoe, Cinderella produced the other glass slipper from her pocket. Before she even slipped her foot into the slipper, the officials knew she was the perfect fit, the rightful recipient. Who else would possess the matching glass slipper but the very one for whom it was made in the first place? And of course, it fit perfectly!

Your daughter is cherished by a far greater Prince, a real one who didn't need to search high and low throughout His kingdom to find her. Her Prince would stop at nothing to seek and save His chosen one! She uniquely *fits* into the perfect pair that she already possesses—the gifts made and fitted precisely for her, the rightful recipient. This is true of all precious princesses, though each one's glass-slipper gift is different and fitted uniquely to her. And *since the glass slipper fits, why not wear it?!* Receiving these gifts and wearing them, your child is *walking* as God's chosen princess, in the roles and the purposes her heavenly Father made uniquely for her, as she uses her gifts in relationship with others and for His glory.

Help your growing girl envision herself now in these custom-fit glass slippers, walking beside a friend down her difficult road, standing by her siblings as they sing together for a good cause, stepping out of her comfort zone to learn a new or scary skill, tiptoeing into the rooms of the elderly to tenderly care for their needs, and gliding gracefully into other people's lives, showing and sharing the love of Jesus that they wouldn't otherwise know. Above all, she is walking in the Word, growing in knowledge and wisdom, so that she can be equipped for His kingdom work for her. Colossians 1:10 tells us to **"walk in a manner worthy of the Lord, fully pleasing to Him, bearing fruit in every good work and increasing in the knowledge of God."**

DON'T CONFORM–BE TRANSFORMED!

Daily, your daughter is surrounded by words, images, and the opinions of others, all attempting to redefine who she is in relation to them. These range from well-meaning family members and teachers to critical ones, from the heroes or heroines of a storybook to the popular posts on social media. Maybe family members or classroom teachers boast of your daughter's accomplishments, and she worries that if she doesn't continue to meet their expectations, she'll cease to be who they think she is or she will no longer be valued. Or what if one of them chooses to make an example of your sweet pea, based on one day's poor performance or behavior? Inadvertently, this person of influence has stamped a label of identity onto her, and she might struggle to scrub it off. Even the hero or protagonist of a favorite story can leave your princess feeling lacking, since she doesn't see herself as capable of a fictional character's amazing accomplishments or brave deeds. Social media is perhaps the most pervasive source of impact, as countless images and ideas flash before her, from friends sharing only their best features, to peers making hateful remarks, to strangers pinning or posting their perfect creations or achievements, to boasting or even bullying. As a result, your little girl may shrink back, questioning her worth or measuring her identity.

It's no wonder many girls will struggle with an identity crisis as they grow from the infants of God's creation into the young women He plans for them to become. The "identity crisis" was coined by developmental psychologist Erik Erikson "to describe the temporary instability and confusion adolescents experience as they struggle with alternatives and choices" (psychology.jrank.org/Identity-Identity-Formation.html [02-01-15]). According to a 2015 article on Family-Lobby.com, the struggle with identity is one of the biggest challenges an adolescent will face during the transition from childhood to adulthood. Where this and every crucial topic about your daughter is concerned, you can be her biggest advocate! Remind her again of God's words in Romans 12:2, looking at them this time in light of her identity: **"Do not be conformed to this world, but be transformed by the renewal**

of your mind, that by testing you may discern what is the will of God, what is good and acceptable and perfect." She doesn't have to be conformed to the world that tries to define her identity based upon cultural expectations and bias. Guide her toward God-pleasing decisions, looking to His Word and seeking His lead as she explores her talents and gifts, so that she'll begin to recognize and discern His will for her life and how she can use them as a part of His perfect plan—to benefit and bless others, to fulfill her future vocation, and to give God glory!

A WORD OF GRACE

I've suffered from an identity crisis more than once; so has my daughter. And so have you. Struggles with identity are not limited to the adolescent years (http://psychology.jrank.org/pages/322/Identity-Identity-Formation.html [02-01-15]). We are especially vulnerable following times of transition, when the people around us have changed, when our surroundings are new and unfamiliar, or when our position or purpose has shifted. It's at these times that we may even wonder, "Who am I?" While it's natural to feel a temporary loss of identity at such times, I think that it happens to me when I have wrapped my identity too tightly around another person or an ability or accomplishment. When I'm no longer recognized or able to achieve what I used to, I begin to wonder what my purpose is. I wonder "Who am I?" and "What is my purpose now?" Maybe you can relate. And maybe, like me, you've been partially responsible for wrapping your daughter's identity solely around something she does or who you perceive her to be in relation to you, and this has left you with a heavy heart.

Take your heavy heart to God, acknowledging and confessing your confusion about your identity and that of your precious princess. He understands that change and transition may have led to these emotional struggles, and He offers you His forgiveness as you come to Him. Your Savior can calm your anxieties, remind you who you are, and affirm your purpose. The One who created you and formed your innermost parts (Psalm 139:13) said, **"Fear not, for I have redeemed you; I have called you by name, you are Mine"** (Isaiah 43:1). He covers you with His grace as He reminds you through His Word that you are His chosen and redeemed child; your identity is found in Him. Cling to the truth that the One who loves you eternally also has a purpose for you, though the details may change throughout your life story. **"The Lord will fulfill His purpose for me; Your steadfast love, O Lord, endures forever. Do not forsake the work of Your hands"** (Psalm 138:8).

SHOW AND TELL

1. Talk about the beginnings of your daughter's life story—how did you first learn about her? Describe your feelings and response when you saw her for the very first time. Show her several Scripture passages that reveal her true identity. Remind her with regular notes, words, and hugs that she is your princess. God's princess. His valued and treasured possession, chosen in Christ, her Savior!

2. What do your words and witness reveal to your daughter regarding your own identity and how you view yourself, your purpose, and your value? Does she hear you cut yourself down because you lack a desired ability? Or do you verbally acknowledge your God-given gifts and use

them? Take a moment to consider and share some of your defining gifts and abilities.

3. Do you realize if or when you've compared yourself to someone else based on appearance or accomplishment? Have you fallen prey to others' words or to their apparent abilities that leave you feeling inadequate? Relate these struggles to the ones your daughter may be having, and ask her these questions too, adapting them to her level of understanding, depending on her age. Encourage her to focus on her God-given gifts and to be grateful for (rather than envious of) others' differing gifts, asking for God's strength to dare not to compare. (And as you do, heed the advice of your own words!)

4. Prayerfully consider how you can continually encourage and impact your daughter regarding her growing gifts and abilities as you simultaneously seek to remind her of her true identity found in Christ!

Chapter 3

Life in the Word, Part One—
In the Palace

And these words that I command you today shall be on your heart.
You shall teach them diligently to your children, and shall talk of
them *when you sit in your house,* and when you walk by the way,
and when you lie down, and when you rise. Deuteronomy 6:6–7
(emphasis added)

GOD'S LIVING AND ACTIVE WORD

With the turn of every page in these earli-
est chapters of your daughter's life story, you can trust
that God continues to cover you with His grace as
you raise her to be a godly girl, secure in her identity,
which is found and formed in Christ. With your gentle
and guiding hand upon her life from the start, you'll
watch your princess grow and change before your
very eyes—sometimes noticeably overnight!—and
you can trust that God will provide you with what
you need to be fully sufficient for this most important
task. And what you'll need, first and foremost, is His
Word—God's living and active Word (Hebrews 4:12).
Already in this book, you've been given a glimpse of

the central role that Scripture plays across every topic covered here as it applies to all of her life—and yours. Now, in this chapter and in the next, we're going to specifically address *life in the Word.*

Do you dream of how your daughter's life story will be lived out? If so, do you envision that it could be one lived in the Word? And what does "life in the Word" even mean? It refers to more than intentional time spent reading and studying the Bible; it's also about life *lived* by it (although time spent regularly reading God's Word is foundational and a large portion of what I address here). Every moment of every day, by God's grace, you can treasure His Word in your heart and teach it to your children by your words and example. That intentionality begins at home in your palace, under your royal roof. Much of our life story is lived out at home, of course (as we read in Deuteronomy 6:7: **"when you sit in your house . . ."**). But before we dive in any further, let's take a look at the bigger picture.

HIS STORY

I've begun each chapter thus far referring to your daughter's life story, but the bigger picture of life as we consider her story, yours, and that of all God's chosen children is really His story, which begins . . . in the beginning.

"In the beginning, God created the heavens and the earth" (Genesis 1:1). The Bible is, in part, a book of history from the very beginning, but more important is that it is HIS story. So much more than words on pages, the Word—the very Word of God—is the world's most significant story. The Scriptures are not an assortment of isolated stories, but one God-breathed, flawless, true story. My husband, who is a pastor, hesitates to use the word *story* when describing Scripture because of his encounters with people who tell him that they grew up learning Bible stories as disconnected, often confusing, accounts that were <u>not</u> taught to them as portions of a complete work. It makes me sad to think that many people see the biblical accounts merely as fascinating or fictional tales. But what are these *stories,* really? They are scenes right out of the bigger picture of continuous history. They are passages, written in both prose and poetry and recorded in this most compelling account for each one of us, with every verse and every chapter working together to point us to Christ. The Bible is one very long and amazing story in which the Creator of the universe reveals His plan of salvation and brings it to fruition through His Son, Jesus Christ, who was sent for the redemption of all sinners—including you and me, your daughter and mine, and our entire royal families. It's the salvation story! Examine every part of your life story, and of your daughter's, in light of God's grace-filled Christ-centered Word.

ON YOUR HEART

The passage from Deuteronomy 6 at the opening of this chapter tells us that His Words "shall be on your heart." And by the Spirit's leading, the desire of our heart is to impress these Words firmly upon our children's hearts too. It's essential that you dig into the Bible and store it in your heart so that you learn the Word of truth, which you have the privilege of sharing and living out by example as you pass on His promises to the next generation.

The Word of God will be on your heart when you hear it proclaimed and read in worship, when you jump into Bible study alone, and as you read your Bible daily in devotion. Philippians 2:16 exhorts us to **"[hold] fast to the word of life,"** that is, to cling to Christ and to His Word, where the Holy Spirit works powerfully to draw you closer. Chapter 9, "Your Presence Is Requested," is devoted to the topic of investing meaningful time with your princess as you build your relationship. It is even more important to invest time in your relationship with the One who created you, redeemed you, and calls you His dear daughter. Ask the Holy Spirit to create in you a desire to spend time in God's Word. Dedicate one-on-one time with your heavenly Father. Open the Bible expectantly, trusting that He meets you there—because He promises you that He will. Open it with a reverent awe. Just think of it: your Lord and Savior chooses to meet with you personally, speaks to you, and guides, strengthens, and comforts you through His Word! When your daughter catches you clinging to the Word and enjoying quiet time with your Savior, when she notices the power His Word has upon your life, she will learn by your example, will want what you have, and will likely emulate you. If she doesn't already have a Bible of her own, one for her personal use makes a wonderful gift.

GOD-BREATHED

As you grow in God's Word and seek to instill it in your princess's life, remember each beautiful portion of this passage: **"All Scripture is breathed out by God and profitable for teaching, for reproof, for correction, and for training in righteousness"** (2 Timothy 3:16). Let these words remind you, as a Bible student and teacher, that every word in the Scriptures is from God. The Holy Spirit works powerfully through all

Scripture, which can fill you with knowledge and understanding of His truth. It can call you to repentance from sin and guide you in living out the righteousness you've been given by God's grace in Christ. God allowed each author—from Moses, to David, to the apostles Paul and John and others—to use their cultural backgrounds and styles and to write within the context of their settings. But the inspiration behind every word comes from God, the ultimate author of it all.

ABSOLUTE TRUTH

Expect opposition to the authority of God's Word. Because the Bible is absolute truth, the final authority for our lives, applicable and relevant, and **"able to make [us] wise for salvation through faith in Christ Jesus"** (2 Timothy 3:15), Satan will try every trick and tactic he can to tell us and our daughters otherwise. He knows our weaknesses and will use every opportunity to cause us to doubt God. Our nemesis may use modern media or pop culture; he may attack through atheistic instructors, skeptical peers, and others who don't know Christ and don't see the need to know Him. But we can be confident because we are armed with God's ever-powerful, changeless, flawless Word (Psalm 18:30), written and recorded to speak to us and our children today in our ever-changing, deeply flawed world. **"Let this be recorded for a generation to come, so that a people yet to be created may praise the Lord"** (Psalm 102:18). Trust God to guide you and strengthen you as you share His absolute truth with your dear daughter.

TEACH AND TALK

Let's look again at the instructions to parents from Deuteronomy 6. With God's Word already on your heart, what, practically speaking, can you do to imprint the Scriptures onto your precious princess's heart, beginning the day she is born and continuing all the while that she resides in your humble palace? Verse 7 tells us to **"teach them diligently to your children, and . . . talk of them when you sit in your house."** It's natural to sit to talk, especially at home as you gather in the comfort of your house, away from days spent "beyond the palace gates." The haven called home is the perfect place to talk about the Lord. Home is where conversation and interaction are as natural as breathing. You and your husband can teach God's Word to your princess as she witnesses the priority of your faith walk with your every breath and action. Recognize and encourage your husband's role as a spiritual leader of the family. (If you are parenting alone or if your husband does not provide spiritual leadership or support you in yours, take heart; the Lord will continue to guide, strengthen, and enable you to impress God's Word powerfully upon your dear daughter's heart.) Let her see that you put Christ at the center.

Life in the Word begins with time together at home and in the Word each day.

DAILY DEVOTION TIME

Please don't throw your hands up in defeat, wondering how you can possibly do this. I've been there. I remember thinking *Isn't* daily *asking too much?* when I had little ones underfoot and I was failing to carve out my own devotion time. Then another mom helped me to look at the nature of life through a different lens. She encouraged me to consider more closely the daily care and provision of my heavenly Father and the subsequent daily care I give my children:

"Blessed be the Lord, who daily bears us up; God is our salvation" (Psalm 68:19). He provides for my daily needs. Jesus instructs me to pray accordingly: **"Give us each day our daily bread"** (Luke 11:3). That means He is the ultimate provider of my children's needs as well, even those I delivered by my hands. He tells us that we are to take that a step further by encouraging others in the faith that they would trust in God too: **"But exhort one another every day, as long as it is called 'today,'"** (Hebrews 3:13). Daily, I have the responsibility *and* the privilege of encouraging my children in their faith. With this at the forefront of my mind, I realized that *daily* family devotion time didn't sound so difficult.

I also learned not to be legalistic about this all-important pursuit. At first, I feared we would miss so many days that we would give up trying altogether. Then, God led me to see that He blessed every opportunity we took to gather around His Word, and He guided us to desire it more. Soon, we found time for devotions on a regular, if not daily, basis.

So what does that look like?

★ *Plan and prepare for devotion time.* **"Teach them diligently to your children"** (Deuteronomy 6:7). Intentionally and diligently look for tools and resources that are most helpful, age-appropriate, and relevant for your daughter and the rest of your family. Seek the help of your pastor or another Christian mom. Look in your church library, search for downloadable and online family devotions, and borrow resources from friends. Shop online and at Christian bookstores. Compare children's Bibles, Bible story books, movies, and news outlets for illustrations and content that suit your needs.

✶ *Schedule a time.* Take a look at your day and week. What time might work best? When your daughter is very young, consider that several brief visits with God throughout the day may be more fitting and feasible than one larger chunk of time. As she matures, find a time that consistently works for you and for her—for the entire family, if possible. If it is bedtime, as it usually was at our house, you're sending your sweetheart to bed with the truth of God's Word and the security of family. Maybe it's at mealtime; maybe it's first thing in the morning, if you sit down to breakfast together. Or maybe it's during daily commute time together. If you find that your initial plan isn't working, simply rearrange your routine until you find a time of day that suits everyone.

★ *Don't give up!* As your daughter grows and changes and as your family juggles differing schedules and commitments, your devotion plans, timing, and materials will need to change. Be willing to adapt. Continue to make this precious time a priority whenever possible.

DEVOTION TIME REVISITED . . . IN OUR PALACE

The following section chronicles my family's devotion time at home during our children's growing-up years. By no means must yours look like ours. Based on your schedule and family dynamics, another approach may work better for you, your precious princess, and the entire royal family.

When our children were very young, I trusted the Holy Spirit was at work in them already as they grew in their baptismal faith, yet I wondered what they'd be able to grasp. We were determined to begin teaching them from the time of their birth, but how could we begin sharing the Word of God as we sat at home? How could we surround their little lives with the love of Jesus? First, we read to them from sturdy Bible board books. We showed them how to fold their little hands to pray, using simple words and short phrases. We praised Jesus with scriptural sing-along tunes and were delighted to hear God's Word echoed by memory through song. One day, clearly delighted, Courtney realized she could spell a second name in addition to her own. Running to me, she cried, "Mommy, mommy! I can spell Jesus!" With her head bobbing back and forth, she sang quite simply, "J-E-S-U-S, and Jesus is His name!"

When our twins were four years old, their dad and I presented them with their very own children's Bibles. Filled with vibrant illustrations and short stories, these Bible story books were instrumental in guiding our family through many Bible narratives for the first (and second!) time. We read them cover to cover. God used this season of our lives in wonderful ways, nurturing faith in me as He did in my little ones. I was amazed at the depth they were able to grasp and was humbled to admit that I'd not known a great number of Bible stories or the chronological events of the Old Testament. I learned alongside my children. This time prepared me, as a result, to dive in deeper on my own because I was no longer lost or intimidated by the scope of it.

During their preschool and kindergarten years, our routine was to read just before bedtime with our little ones on our laps. As our children moved into and through their elementary years, our family continued to try new age-appropriate, even challenging, resources. With a more in-depth children's Bible in their hands, they often led us in evening devotion time. They wouldn't let us miss it! Every story ended with questions and application for *their* life stories. Before long, we handed them youth Bibles that contained the complete Scriptures, and we encouraged them to read on their own.

Also, over the years, we curled up with picture books and chapter books containing biblical messages and themes, including Christian fiction series such as The Chronicles of Narnia, which my children loved well into their teen years. Every resource opened the door for discussion, insight, and the opportunity to talk about our faith on a personal level.

As years passed, we had a hard time staying with one devotion book, so we designated a basket to hold several Bibles and thematic devotionals designed to address the questions, concerns, and needs of today's teen. Our variety basket sat on the floor of the living room, and we took turns choosing and reading aloud from a resource it held.

This worked well for a while, but gradually, conflicting schedules kept us from continuing on a daily basis, and there were times I felt like a failure. I was afraid that we were giving up this privileged time entirely. I worried that our earlier efforts wouldn't be remembered or repeated. But God is faithful, even in my worries, fears, and failures. Our children were growing in the Word in other ways, right under our royal roof, through movies and music viewed and played in our home and through books they'd grown to love. Only later did I learn that Courtney had been selecting the teen devotionals from the variety basket for daily devotion time of her own.

Recently, Courtney called home from college. She attends a Christian university and studies the Scriptures on a regular basis for a few of her classes. On this day, one class in particular gave her pause. As she was working through her curriculum, she realized *I know all these stories.* "Mom," she said with emotion, "you've taught them to me since I was little. From the start. I want to be a parent like that!" I'm not sure I responded audibly because of the lump in my throat. Although I didn't always feel faithful, although at times I doubted and fretted over what I should have done differently, God was faithful through His Word and worked through my humble efforts to **"talk of them"** as we sat in our little palace.

AS YOU SIT IN YOUR PALACE . . .

★ It is never too early or too late to start. I've shared our family's limited stash of ideas from their toddler to teen years, but it's never too late to begin devotions together, even if your daughter is a tween or a teen already.

★ If you are new to the Christian faith or don't know a lot about the Bible, that's okay! You can learn alongside your growing girl, as I did, and you may choose to use a study Bible of your own to increase your understanding and ability to teach her.

★ Use technology to your advantage. Access the Bible on your smartphone or tablet; download useful apps, online family devotions, video clips with relevant messages, or other helpful materials.

★ Perhaps you will discover, as I did, that when you are diligent with your time together, it becomes a routine, and children thrive on a routine. It's likely, then, that your sweet girl will not let you forget devotion time. Even if your committed time is brief, take it! Share a nugget of God's precious Word, and watch it make a difference in the next pages of her life story.

✴ When your royalty is ready, allow her to take a turn leading devotions. Challenge her by quizzing her, or let her pose questions to you when devotions are ending.

✴ Devotion time doesn't have to be complicated or lengthy. In fact, I used a rule of thumb that worked for our family on many occasions: *Keeping it simple will keep it happening.* Trust that the Holy Spirit is working powerfully through the Word of God as it's shared in any fashion. Trust that He is working in the hearts of every member of the family. God promises that His Word will accomplish His purposes, and it is always God's desire that we and our children grow in faith: **"So shall My word be that goes out from My mouth; it shall not return to Me empty, but it shall accomplish that which I purpose, and shall succeed in the thing for which I sent it"** (Isaiah 55:11).

AS SHE STORES IT IN HER HEART

As you pore over God's Word together, impressing it upon your daughter, and especially as your growing girl begins to study it on her own, share with her the bigger picture. His story—all of Scripture—points to Christ, whether she's reading history, prophecy, or poetry and whether she has opened her Bible to the Old or New Testament. Wherever she reads, she's **"grow[ing] in the grace and knowledge of our Lord and Savior Jesus Christ"** (2 Peter 3:18). Remind her that the Bible is much more than words on a page (in contrast with every other book she opens). It is living and active (Hebrews 4:12), and God the author is with her, speaking through the passages. The Holy Spirit moves powerfully through them to work in her life story. She may wrestle with difficult portions; some will lead her to ask questions and others will confuse her. Some will offer clear direction right away, and still others will give her immediate peace. In each response, gently remind her that she can trust His every Word. Teach her to apply the Bible to every situation in her life. Her worldview is formed by the truth she learns and believes! When difficult decisions, tough circumstances, or powerful temptations parade before her, she will be equipped to stand up under them with a firm grasp of right and wrong and the ability to discern between the two as she views each situation through the lens of God's Word.

As a young adult now, my daughter shares with me the amazing events that often follow her time in the Word. Sometimes, the very verse or passage she's just read leads quite unexpectedly to an observation or revelation connected to a conversation or event she is involved with. What follows is the opportunity to share it or apply it, to receive direction or discernment, while praising Him for the Spirit's work through the Word.

ON THE DOORPOSTS AND ON YOUR GATES

You've read much in this chapter about teaching and talking at home. Now, before we step outside the palace door and go beyond the gates (or literally turn the page to the next chapter) to look at *Life in the Word* "out there," let's examine another verse that is also a part of this parenting passage: **"Write them on the doorposts of your house and on your gates"** (Deuteronomy 6:9). In other words, you are to keep God's Word ever before you as a continual reminder of His lordship over your family's life, as a witness to all who enter, and as a beautiful reminder of His grace in Christ Jesus and the salvation that you have in Him. Try some of these ideas:

* Choose a family theme verse that you print and post on the front of your fridge or frame for everyone to see. A couple of verses to consider include **"But as for me and my house, we will serve the Lord"** (Joshua 24:15) and **"For I know the plans I have for you, declares the Lord, plans for welfare and not for evil, to give you a future and a hope"** (Jeremiah 29:11).

* Play Christian music in your home. What an effective and fun means to memorize Scripture, lighten hearts, and encourage positive choices in lyrics and music for years to come. Enjoy Christian music in a variety of genres, including (but not limited to) kids' sing-along songs, hymns and worship music, contemporary music, and rock. Consider the impact and the influence your choice of music can have, not only upon your family, but upon everyone who enters your home.

* Handwrite Bible verses, and post them to the bathroom mirror. Tuck them on your princess's pillow. Pack them in her lunch. Share bits of God's Word in every place possible. Think thematically: **"O, taste and see that the Lord is good!"** (Psalm 34:8)—on the pantry. **"A glad heart makes a cheerful face"** (Proverbs 15:13)—on a mirror. **"Train up a child in the way he should go; even when he is old he will not depart from it"** (Proverbs 22:6)—on the children's or family Bible.

* Post a question of the week, such as: "If you could jump into Bible history, what scene would you want to see?" "What's your favorite verse?" "Think of someone from the Bible whose name starts with the same letter as yours and talk about him or her." Ask biblical-values-based questions that help her think through virtues such as honesty, integrity, and purity.

✴ Perhaps your palace décor can include scriptural art, a cross, a picture of Christ, or other expressions of your faith. Let them serve as constant reminders of the Savior whom you serve and the love you have in Him!

DON'T CONFORM—BE TRANSFORMED!

Life in the Word is a life of dependence upon God. And that flies in the face of modern-day culture, which attempts to train us and our children to be self-made people, kings and queens of our own destiny. I recently read a Facebook post that told me I should not wait for a prince to ride in on his white horse to rescue me from my struggles or my sins because I can be my own savior-of-sorts. The words turned my stomach. Each of us is in desperate need of a Savior, and we certainly won't find it within ourselves or from some guy riding a horse. The truth is, there is only One who can save us; Christ Jesus, our Prince of Peace, is our Rescuer. Our Savior. And this truth is at the center of God's Word of life. That's why life in the Word is critical. The Word reminds us, **"Do not be conformed to this world, but be transformed by the renewal of your mind, that by testing you may discern what is the will of God, what is good and acceptable and perfect"** (Romans 12:2). While the world may tell your daughter that she doesn't need the Bible and attempt to lure her into believing the Bible is outdated or irrelevant or merely the words of man, you know better. And you're teaching her the truth as you sit together in your house, reverently talking about Jesus and guiding her into the Bible over and over. Show her by your life that you are dependent upon God for everything. Then trust Him to work in her heart and yours, as He transforms you both through His Word, the very means by which you may discern His **"good and acceptable and perfect"** will!

A WORD OF GRACE

How many times have I needed a word of grace when I've berated myself over another day's failure to spend time in God's Word or share it with my dear daughter? I'm guessing you've been there too. Maybe it has been months or even years since you opened the Bible.

The Holy Spirit nudges us. We know we need time with the Lord. Or do we? Do we excuse away our lack of time in His Word because we fail to recognize the power of God in it, the strength we receive from it, or the guidance and direction we are given in it? Do we tell ourselves that we have other priorities right now? How comforting it is to know that we can confess these and every one of our shortcomings to God, ask Him for a new or renewed commitment to give Him our time, and receive His loving words of grace. God assures us: **"The steadfast love of the LORD never ceases; His mercies never come to an end; they are new every morning; great is Your faithfulness"** (Lamentations 3:22–23). His mercies never end; they are brand new every day! And with each new day comes a new opportunity to follow the Spirit's nudge to grow in the Word and share it, to receive His strength, guidance, and direction, and to be renewed by His grace and mercy!

SHOW AND TELL

1. Take stock of a typical day. When could you carve out time to grow in the Word? In order to make time on a regular basis, take a look at your discretionary time

and determine what could be traded in, if possible. For example, say no to another commitment or give up your least favorite must-see TV show. Explore options for devotional resources and glean ideas from other people. Open the Bible with great expectations, trusting God will speak to you there! Model for your sweet princess a life in the Word, at home in the palace.

2. Recall the basics I shared as you seek to begin (or begin again) family devotions:
   a. Plan and prepare for devotion time.
   b. Schedule a time.
   c. Don't give up! Try a new time, method, or location, as necessary.

3. What will your planning and preparation include as you search for resources and consider your daughter's age and needs? What is the best possible time to try first? What backup plans can you have in place so you'll not be tempted to give up as your family's schedule varies and your needs change?

4. As you show Jesus to your growing girl and tell her all about His saving love, remember that you are merely the messenger, the vessel that God uses to faithfully share His Word and His ways. He is the one who changes hearts. He sends His Holy Spirit to create, grow, and strengthen faith. Trust His work in her life as you remain the faithful messenger of His grace. Where have you seen evidence of her growing faith as you sit in your palace together?

5. How significant do you perceive your role of raising your daughter to be, according to God's Word? Read 2

Timothy 1:5; 3:14–15. In these verses, the apostle Paul commends and encourages Timothy in his faith, relating it directly to the sincere faith of his mother and grandmother, who shared the Scriptures with Timothy from childhood. How do these verses speak to you, regarding your role, your opportunities, and your potential impact? As you are guided by God's grace, what is one new way you can encourage your princess to continue in what she has learned and has firmly believed (see 2 Timothy 3:14) as she has learned it from you?

Chapter 4

Life in the Word, Part Two—
Beyond the Palace Gates

These words that I command you today shall be on your heart.
You shall teach them diligently to your children, and shall talk of
them when you sit in your house, and *when you walk by the way*.
Deuteronomy 6:6–7 (emphasis added)

WALK BY THE WAY

$\mathcal{L}$*ife in the Word* begins at home in the
palace, as you talk about and live out God's Word. It's
the place where many, many pages of your family members' life stories are written. But what happens when
you're not at home? Notice what else our Deuteronomy directive says about parents teaching their children:
"talk of them . . . when you walk by the way." When
God gave Moses these commands to impart upon His
people, most travel was done via feet. Families would
"walk by the way" for every purpose and destination.
Yes, you and your princess can have great talks about
God as you walk hand in hand or side by side. But you
also "walk by the way" whenever and however you
travel together every time you leave your home.

Impressing God's Word upon our offspring is so important that we are to teach it diligently at all times, when we are at home and when we're not. As queen of the palace, you manage the affairs of the entire royal family within the walls of your home—and often outside them as well. (Read Proverbs 31 for affirmation!) Where do you spend time when you are not at home, and what can life in the Word look like beyond the palace gates?

CHURCH TIME

Church is the most important destination beyond the walls of your home. It is the place to which you take your precious children to be baptized into God's family by faith and the place where everyone in your family grows in faith as they hear the Word together! Regular church time is essential in the faith life of your royal family.

You and your husband are not on this mission alone; your church family partners with you to "teach [the Word] diligently" to your children. If you struggle to make worship and Sunday School attendance a regular commitment or priority in your life right now, consider the benefits that far outweigh any reason for not steering the family carriage toward the church on Sunday. Benefits of worship include

- the Means of Grace: hearing the Word read and proclaimed and receiving the Sacrament of Holy Communion for the forgiveness of sins, and

- fellowship: singing praises to God, lifting your voices in prayer with other believers, and obtaining encouragement and affirmation from other parents and families.

"And let us consider how to stir up one another to love and good works, not neglecting to meet together, as is the habit of some, but encouraging one another, and all the more as you see the Day drawing near" (Hebrews 10:24–25). You also receive Christ's strength for the days ahead, fortifying you against the assaults of the evil one, the temptations of the world, and the weaknesses of your own sinful flesh.

What a privilege you and I have to lead our children to worship, especially as we consider that every day is one day closer to the glorious day of Christ's return!

As a regular churchgoing habit is instilled, don't be surprised if your children say something similar to these words of the psalmist: **"I was glad when they said to me, "Let us go to the house of the LORD!"** (Psalm 122:1). I remember our little prince and princess chiming together, "We get to go to church, we get to go to church!" Make church special. Prepare ahead. Celebrate when Sunday comes. Persist through the preteen years when you may hear a few sighs and groans. Revel in the teen years, trusting that God's Word is working in this and every stage of her life story, even if it appears that she isn't engaged. Gathered together in God's house, strengthened in the Word and the Sacraments, and encouraged by other believers, you and your family receive eternal benefits.

A LIFE OF WORSHIP

We hear alarming statistics telling us that the current generation is leaving the church in droves. Our evil nemesis delights in using these so-called statistics just to make us give up and assume our children will become a part of them. Again and again, I see heartwarming evidence to the contrary.

And where do I see it? In the families who intentionally, by God's grace, make church a priority while their kids are growing up. I see it when the king and queen of the family palace faithfully lead their growing royalty through the doors of church on a regular basis, not out of compulsion but out of joy! And I see it in the families that don't view church as something they have to do on Sunday, but as an expression of a life in the Word, a life of daily worship, where teaching and talking are a natural part of life, in response to the Holy Spirit's work in their lives. This life of worship can continue, generation after generation, only by God's grace!

YOUR ATTITUDE SPEAKS VOLUMES

It's never too early, and it's never too late to start! Maybe your baby daughter is still living out the opening pages of her life story. I encourage you to begin taking her to church now. Yes, pack the diaper bag and strap her into her car seat even during the difficult infant and toddler years when you wonder if you'll ever make it through a service without constant distractions, spills, or tears (yours AND hers!). Children soon learn how to behave and how to participate in the worship service.

Your attitude speaks volumes to her, even when it seems she's too small to notice and even when she's a preteen with an attitude of her own. As one perceptive child shared, "Kids can tell if their parents want to be [in church], if they're excited about ministry. We kids look to our parents so much about how to act and how to feel." Are you excited or apathetic? The combination of your eager attitude as you prepare for church and your reverent attitude throughout the service will go a long way toward shaping your little one into a wee worshiper who looks forward to going to God's house. It will go even further toward molding your not-so-little one into a regular worshiper who continues to go to God's house, even when she no longer lives in *your* house. To be honest, there were weeks when my attitude was not what it should have been; I didn't want to let it show, but then felt guilty for "putting on a good face" and feeling like a hypocrite. I prayed that God would change my heart. I was humbled, time and again, when my attitude made a U-turn during worship. And even when my attitude was only marginally improved, I knew that I had followed God's will by going to church, and by His grace, I left worship fed, forgiven, and strengthened for the week ahead.

A dear friend of mine is busily juggling four small children, the youngest still a babe in arms. She and her husband have determined to do all they can to consistently give priority and time to worship in church, and they're quite deliberate in their approach. They gently define expectations for behavior well before they arrive, explaining the desire to give God their best as they arrive at church. They even practice church at home (what a novel idea!). The kids think it's great fun when they line up chairs and practice sitting and standing while learning what it is like to worship as a family, giving praise to God and receiving His good gifts. This king and queen are imparting an attitude for worship to their young royal family that will not be forgotten.

ANTICS IN THE PEW

During a recent trip to speak at a women's retreat, I stayed with a special young pastor's family, and I was blessed to enjoy the energy and affection of their three young children.

On Sunday morning, I accompanied them to church. From the front seat of their minivan, I turned to talk to them, thinking that I would cleverly encourage some good behavior in regard to the upcoming church service. I said, "I'm so excited to sit with your family in church today because your mom has told me that you all sit and listen so well, giving God your worship!" Silence. Three serious expressions. Finally, the rambunctious three-year-old replied, "Well . . . maybe you'd better sit somewhere else." And what did I see in the pew a few minutes later? Little ones whose hands were busy and whose feet fidgeted, but whose voices chimed in during the songs and whose faces lit up at the mention of David and Goliath in Daddy's sermon. These little ones were listening from the middle of an active pew!

My husband and I tried not to let our pew become a three-ring circus full of food and activities, but we did provide a few quiet options, particularly when our royal subjects were young enough that the length of their attention span did not correspond to the length of the worship service. When they were beginning to read, I pointed to the words in the hymnal, the bulletin, or the song sheet, gently letting them know where we were as I taught and encouraged them to follow along. Don't underestimate what your precious princess is able to understand and learn in worship, even as a small child, as the Holy Spirit guides and grows her faith.

BEYOND THE WORSHIP SERVICE

Find out what your congregation offers your growing girl and the rest of your family. Ask about Bible studies or parent classes where you may connect with other moms and dads, glean from seasoned parents who have led their families down similar paths, and grow in your role as parent. Seek answers from the pastor and other parents. Find out: Is there a midweek family ministry? What about Sunday School? A children's choir or praise team? Vacation Bible School? Puppet ministry? Youth group, Bible study, MOPS, small group ministry, or other opportunity? Do these groups meet on Sunday morning, throughout the week, or less frequently?

Maybe you're thinking, "That sounds like a lot of church stuff. Isn't Sunday morning enough?" Our daughters are faced with so many options for their time and attention. As we help them discover and explore their gifts, we may commit them to a vast variety of good activities, from dance to athletics to music and more. While each endeavor may be quite worthwhile, sometimes the sheer number of activities divides family time and attention and minimizes opportunities for faith growth as well. How can we cautiously choose the direction and number of commitments we'll make? Prayerfully consider making the church a place of *primary* involvement. There, your family finds community with other believers and a center of social life. There, you can connect with other God-fearing families, and your daughter can meet like-minded peers. And there, she will be blessed with opportunities that involve her not only spiritually and socially, but also educationally and recreationally as she learns about the love of Jesus in as many settings as possible within the church.

MINISTRY AND MISSIONS
What a blessing in the faith life of your family when you not only fill the pews and the classrooms, but also step up to serve in the ministry of your church. Encourage your daughter to join you in whatever ways she can as you use your gifts

to serve. She'll gain a heart for helping others and grow in her desire to spend time at church in a variety of capacities. She'll have opportunities to explore, discover, and practice using her unique gifts. Perhaps she could play a piano solo before service, help you set up for a bake sale, assist in the nursery, write a Bible skit, or help deliver meals to those in need. Your example to your dear daughter is monumental, especially as she sees you serve with joy!

When our children were young, God filled me with a passion for children and family ministries. And my daughter came with me, assisting with set-up, creating props, and helping start a puppet ministry team for our church's "Family Time Bible Study," in which she and others acted out Bible dramas. Before long, she had grown into assisting with and leading other areas of ministry. Youth group, which started in middle school, brought with it an explosion of opportunities in music ministry, community service, Bible study, and even an overseas mission trip. Courtney shared, "Our youth mission trip to Slovakia was an eye-opening hands-on mission experience, a good step in strengthening my faith and also a deciding factor for what I want to do with my life. I learned it's not about me. It's about loving God's people and showing them they're important. They need Jesus, and I learned that I can make a difference. One person can have a huge impact."

Following the mission trip, I asked Courtney and the other girls from the team to give a presentation at our church's women's retreat. As we served together in this special ministry, Courtney and I had the opportunity to use a shared gift we'd each discovered: writing! In a devotion book created for the retreat, Courtney contributed the following, which spoke of her recognized need to live a life in the Word:

"Is that Bob Marley on your T-shirt?"

"Uh, no, that's Jesus."

"Oh, so you're a Christian?" the boy asked me.

"Absolutely."

He hesitated. "I'm kind of a Christian. I like the principles and everything. But some of it is just so hard to believe."

"What's so hard to believe?" one of my friends chirped in. "That Jesus died and rose? That God made us?"

"How can the world be so black and white to you?" he said defensively in response. "For me, it's all gray."

I was frantically searching my mind for an appropriate response, internally freaking out because nothing was coming to mind. We were at cross-country practice, and Coach was telling us to circle up for stretches. I had to say something fast. So I hurriedly said the best response that came to mind: "Gray reminds me of old people!"

Okay. That was so lame. And not very nice. But it was all that I could come up with. During practice, I kept hitting my head against the proverbial wall, accusing myself. *Why couldn't you come up with a good answer? You just blew a chance at witnessing! What kind of response was that?*

That day reminded me of 1 Peter 3:15, which tells us to **"always [be] prepared to make a defense to anyone who asks you for a reason for the hope that is in you."** If only I had been prepared with a good answer, things might have turned out differently. I will never know.

None of us ever knows when a chance to witness will arise, but we know that we should be prepared for whatever time the opportunity comes up. We don't have to have all the answers, but we should know what we're standing for. We've got to tell all these searching people about the hope we have in Christ, and we can't expect the right words to just pop into our mouths every time. We need to be prepared. We need to be in His Word.

I'm so glad God has grace for everyone, including those who really mess up their witnessing opportunities (a.k.a. me)! When you miss the chance to witness, or just really mess up, know that God is not done with you; He can still use you to **"go . . . and make disciples"** (Matthew 28:19).

Dear Jesus, please give me words to speak when I am asked about my faith and hope in You. Please use me to reach out to those who don't know You. And thanks for the forgiveness You give when I mess up. In Your name, Amen.

Beyond the palace gates lies a land full of teaching opportunities! Outside of church, ministry, and missions, where else do we **"walk by the way"**? Where and how can we teach God's Word diligently and talk about it, incorporating it into every aspect of daily life?

Here are some suggestions. The following "times" provide a wealth of options to consider, enabling you to begin or continue thinking along these lines. Please consider which might work best for you and your family, and don't be overwhelmed by the scope of them.

We "walk by the way" when we travel. Just as the first hearers of this Deuteronomy verse would have spent many hours walking together, traveling by foot, so we travel by carriage (a.k.a. the family car). How do you use this time? How could you make the most of it? Our family spends a lot of time in the car because we live far from our extended families. Like most people, we've had many 15-minute treks in the royal carriage too. How can we use this time to continually nurture our children's faith and share God's truth with them?

★ Car time can provide great talk time! From the comfort of the car seat or the passenger seat, your daughter may feel free to ask faith-based questions and share openly from her heart. Some of our most serious chats have taken place in the car. Confined to a relatively small space with electronics kept in check, we have time and opportunity to share and respond.

★ Look for teachable moments from the world outside the windows. The homeless man by the side of the road: "Let's pray for him. How can we help the hungry in our community? What does God's Word say about helping the poor?" Bumper stickers and billboards: "Is this God-pleasing? Maybe we should pray right now for the people responsible for this message."

★ Listen to positive and Christian music while traveling. Not only can the music you select impact what your impressionable girl may choose later, but your choices give you the opportunity to talk about why you consciously decide not to listen to some secular music, since lyrics, good or bad, are subconsciously memorized and played over and over in the brain. If long trips mean popping in an audio book or a movie, make family-friendly choices and intentionally talk about them. Whenever possible, opt away from individual headsets and personal devices or set a time limit for their use, explaining your desire to enjoy your travel time together.

VACATION TIME

One of our vacations took us to Williamsburg, Virginia, where we read many faith-filled quotes by our founding fathers and enjoyed rich discussion as a result. Hiking in the Black Hills of South Dakota gave us an opportunity to talk about God's creation as we observed the layers of rocks and refuted the evolutionary dating of the earth with the historical record in God's Word. And right there, we praised Him for His handiwork. **"All that is in the heavens and in the earth is Yours. Yours is the kingdom, O Lord, and You are exalted as head above all"** (1 Chronicles 29:11). Look for talking points and teachable moments wherever you travel, whether it's across the country or to the neighborhood park; ask God to guide your conversation in every destination, that you may find within your surroundings a faith-building illustration or teachable moment. Vacation time can also provide the adventure of searching out a church to visit during your travels. Expect God to delight you with His promises in this sanctuary home away from home.

FAMILY WORK TIME

Whether it's weekend yard work or serving in your community or church, working together to the glory of God promotes a Christian work ethic, teaches life skills, and models to your daughter the value of doing her best (see Colossians 3:23). It also models putting others' needs first, working as a team, and being willing to help, which might mean volunteering at a shelter or a camp, shoveling snow for an elderly neighbor, or cleaning up after a church event, as well as countless other possibilities. Talk about why you're serving, and pray together for those you serve. Talk about God's Word while you work, using each specific scenario as an open door of opportunity for teachable moments. Show her what it is to be the hands and feet of Christ, serving with a thankful heart in His name. **"And whatever you do, in word or deed, do everything in the name of the Lord Jesus, giving thanks to God the Father through Him"** (Colossians 3:17). Find the fun in working together!

SPECIAL TIMES

Intentionally seek out special times. Look for Christian musicals, plays, and performances in your area. During the Advent and Lenten seasons, many churches and community groups offer events like *A Walk through Bethlehem*, a *Live Christmas Tree*, or a *Passion Play*. Keep your eyes peeled for Christian concerts, family Bible camps and retreats, Christian comedians, and more. Then be prepared to talk about each and every experience, as God uses these special times and opportunities to touch your daughter's life and yours.

OUT-AND-ABOUT TIME

What an adventure—and a challenge—to recognize that any time you and your daughter are out and about together may become a teaching time, right in the middle of everyday life. A trip to the grocery store, an excursion to the ice cream shop's drive-through lane, and even a detour to the doctor's office can serve to impact her life for Christ. Maybe you help an elderly shopper reach for the groceries on the top shelf; you "pay it forward" for the person behind you in the drive-through lane, passing along the message, "Jesus loves you"; or you answer the receptionist's curt question with a smile and a cheerful word of thanks. Teachable moments exist down every road you walk together as you share God's love.

As queen of your humble palace, you have endless opportunities, by God's grace, to train up your princess to see all of her life, at home and beyond, from a biblical worldview. As God's truth permeates her life, she'll recognize her true identity, purpose, needs, and opportunities in light of His life-giving Word.

DON'T CONFORM—BE TRANSFORMED!

"Do not be conformed to this world, but be transformed by the renewal of your mind, that by testing you may discern what is the will of God, what is good and acceptable and perfect" (Romans 12:2). You are already living counterculturally as you teach the Bible and train up your child within the perimeters of your palace, but your life screams nonconformity when you dare to take His Word outside your home and into every portion of your life. By the power of the Holy Spirit, you are emboldened to speak openly about your faith as you serve neighbors in your community, as you help instructors in your child's school, as you assist colleagues in your work, and more. Seek ways you and your daughter can both be involved at church and in the mission field, across the street or around the world, with the desire to share Jesus wherever He leads you. Expect God's Word to continue to transform you and your growing girl as you live for Him and in service to others. This is completely countercultural in a world that teaches people to live for and serve themselves. God will use your life in the Word to change the world; others can learn of God's will for them in Christ Jesus through you!

A WORD OF GRACE

The distractions of our fast-paced world, especially beyond the palace gates, can cause us to neglect or lose sight of our quest to raise a godly girl. Maybe we've made excuses not to go to church or our attitude from the pew isn't always what it should be. Perhaps we've opted for the path of least resistance as we walk by the way because it's easier to be distracted by our own thoughts than to intentionally look for teachable moments and interact about our faith with our princess and others. Whatever our shortcomings, we know we haven't lived up to the life in the Word that God desires for us. Nevertheless, He desires our best. He gave His best to us when He sent us Christ. We can confess our distractions, excuses, and poor attitudes to our Savior, laying them at the foot of His cross where He laid down His life for every one of our shortcomings. Rest in His mercy. Be confident in His free gift of forgiveness. Receive the strength of the Spirit for a new attitude, fresh zeal, and renewed passion in your quest to raise royalty, by His grace.

SHOW AND TELL

1. What kind of questions do you need to ask to find out how you, your daughter, and your entire family can become involved in church, a prioritized place where you (with the assistance of others) get to teach diligently

as you "walk by the way"? If you're already involved, prayerfully consider where you can best serve or how you can become more active in the church's ministry. How can your daughter come alongside you or serve in her own capacity?

2. Ask God to open your eyes to teachable moments when you go beyond the palace gates with your daughter, that you may be alert and attentive to every opportunity to share God's truth and talk about your faith in Him during travel time, vacation time, family work time, and any other time you are together.

3. What specific thing can you do this week to create an opportunity for talk time about the Lord when you're out and about? When you do, don't worry about every word coming out just right. Simply share from your heart to hers.

4. Your daughter often emulates you, especially as she observes your demeanor, your attitude, and your treatment of others when you are beyond the palace gates, "walking by the way" together. Make it a habit to check your attitude when you're with your daughter. If your demeanor or actions are negative, ask the Lord to guide you to a more positive place, that He may show His love and grace through you.

Chapter 5

Before the Throne—
Approaching the King of Kings in Prayer

Let us then with confidence draw near to the throne of grace,
that we may receive mercy and find grace to help in time of need.
Hebrews 4:16

HELP IN TIME OF NEED

*W*hat's happening right now, on this page of your life story? Of your daughter's life story? Whatever it is, have you taken it to God in prayer? Did you know that because you are draped in Christ's royal robe of righteousness by faith (see Isaiah 61:10 and Philippians 3:9), you—a child of the King of kings—can come to His throne of grace with confidence? There you will find rest in His grace and mercy that covers and cleanses every last one of your sins. And as the words of Hebrews 4:16 (above) reassure you, it's also at His throne of grace you'll receive "help in time of need." And when is that "time of need" for you? for your daughter? for others? Now! Cry out on their behalf and on your own. By the power of the Holy Spirit, you can acknowledge your dependence on God for all things and trust in His perfect provision (Philippians 4:19). You can praise Him for His continual presence (Psalm 105:4) that enables you to approach His throne anytime, anywhere, about anything. You can even ask boldly for His wisdom and discernment for every decision (James 1:5) you make, including those related to raising your growing girl. Rest in the knowledge that the God of the universe cares about every detail of your life; He desires that you bring it to Him and delights in answering, according to His perfect will.

PRAYER IN THESE DAYS

Jesus taught His disciples how to pray, and He lived a life of constant communication with the Father. **"In these days [Jesus] went out to the mountain to pray, and all night he continued in prayer to God"** (Luke 6:12). What had been happening "in these days"? In these early days of His ministry, Jesus was already healing, teaching, and showing compassion to the people around Him. He was being questioned by the legalistic religious leaders, who were already looking for reasons to kill Him. What else was Jesus doing "in these days"? As we see in Luke 6:12, He was going to the Father in prayer, in conversation that continued all night long. He knew the rigors of His ministry in the preceding days and what lay ahead the very next day. Important decisions were to be made. He would minister to multitudes while again healing, teaching, and giving compassion. So in the midst of "these days," Jesus made prayer a first priority.

Jesus did what you and I desperately need to do in *these* days, right here on these pages of our life stories; right now in the rigors of our days. We go to the Lord in prayer. Maybe our conversation won't continue all night long, but it can. He who neither slumbers nor sleeps (Psalm 121:4) is alert to our every word, our every need, day and night. He knows what you and your daughter have just been through; He knows exactly what lies ahead. Take everything to Him, **"for the eyes of the Lord are on the righteous, and His ears are open to their prayer"** (1 Peter 3:12). Yes, it's true. His eyes are always upon us and He calls us righteous, but not because of our own ability or obedience. We are stained by our sin. Our attempts to become righteous by our good deeds are futile; to the Lord, our efforts are no more than filthy rags or polluted garments, as Isaiah 64:6 describes. Christ took our filthy rags upon Himself at the cross and draped over us His royal robe of righteousness (Isaiah 61:10). We are made right with God by His grace through faith in our Savior!

Envision yourself robed in it now, because you are!

What incredible comfort to know that God sees you through Christ's covering of perfection. He is always with you; He listens to your prayers. Come to your heavenly Father's throne of grace!

THE MAGIC WAND OF PRAYER?

Maybe a "magic wand of prayer" sounds ridiculous to you (and it is), but hear me out. In fact, I encourage you to use this illustration to engage your princess in conversation about prayer.

As you draw near with confidence to the King of king's throne of grace, have you treated prayer like a fairy tale's magic wand? Have you hoped that someone would just wave a magic wand of prayer in front of God, and He would instantly take away all your struggles or make all your dreams come true? Cinderella's fairy godmother used her magic wand to create immediate transformation, which culminated with Cinderella's rags turning into a glorious ball gown! And who wouldn't desire transformation like that? These changes enabled a future princess, forgotten and forsaken by her family, to pursue her dreams.

I believe the concept of a magic wand of prayer appeals to us because it would promise instant gratification of our selfish desires. We want it waved at the time and in the way that we believe will benefit us, according to our narrow and shortsighted scope, according to our dreams. We want to be in control, but do we know, in the grander, wide-angle view of life, what's best for us or for our little princesses? We've asked for our dreams to come true, so where are they? *God, didn't You hear? Why didn't You immediately respond to my wish or my daughter's wish (with a YES)?*

In His wisdom, the Lord's answer may be "YES, My child. Yes, and even more abundantly than you can imagine!" (Although you might not recognize it at first!) Then again, His answer may be "NO, because that is not what's best for you or your daughter, even though you desperately want it right now." Or "WAIT—I'm working in others, just as I'm working in you, to accomplish something far greater—in My time, for your good, and for My purpose."

God's ways are better: **"For My thoughts are not your**

thoughts, neither are your ways My ways, declares the
LORD. For as the heavens are higher than the earth, so are
My ways higher than your ways and My thoughts than your
thoughts" (Isaiah 55:8–9).

Trust that God hears every prayer, whether eloquently word-
ed or whispered, sobbed out or said silently. He knows your
struggles and your frustrations. He feels your anger and your
hurt. He is at work in your circumstances and in you. Unlike
Cinderella's pitiful family, He cannot *forget* you; He will
not *forsake* you. He *forgives* you for your selfish desires.
Remember, He has traded your rags for His royal robe, and
that's a far more glorious garment than any old ball gown!
(And by the way, your real-life story of miraculous salvation in Christ is incomparably better and sweeter than any
make-believe tale of magic and dreams come true.)

MAKING THE TIME

If the Lord's ears are open to your every prayer (and they
are!), and if He tells you to come to His throne of grace (and
He does!), then let me ask you: Are you taking the time for
prayer? Are you *making* the time? I may think that I don't
have one minute to spare as I manage the affairs of my palace
and my royal family. My schedule might scream in agreement.
But when I look back to my most rigorous days, I admit that
I still made time for the things I deemed most important. Did
that include prayer? *Ouch.*

Just as we might do when making time for God's Word,
maybe we could consider something of lesser importance that
we can give up in order to find the time for this priority and
privilege. Maybe we can trade in a few minutes of social-
media surfing, a favorite TV show, or a task on our endless

to-do lists for some invaluable prayer time. Making time for prayer sounds so simple and yet so difficult. Much more naturally, we fall into the habit of "doing" first because we're wired (especially as busy moms) to think that productivity equals accomplishment equals value in our day. So let's think of it this way: the time we invest in prayer yields far greater results, by the power of God, than any activity we can complete and cross off our to-do list today. We can thank Him for His forgiveness of our misplaced priorities and our failure to pray and ask Him for a new or renewed desire to make time for the priority and privilege of prayer.

PRAY CONTINUALLY

In Romans 12:12, the apostle Paul urges us to **"be constant in prayer."** Constant. *Really?* In 1 Thessalonians 5:17, he mentions praying continually. How is this possible for busy moms like you and me? Are we supposed to stop everything and pray all night and all day?

While we can and should make time and set aside time for focused prayer, we can also pray in the middle of every detail of life. Consider again the continual presence of the Lord in our lives. He desires that we would be mindful of His presence as we go about our days, trusting in His lead and resisting the sinful desire to attempt to operate in our own strength. By His power at work in our lives, our desire instead is to live with a continual attitude of dependence upon Him and prayer to Him. As you climb into the carriage, as you prepare a feast, and as you scrub the palace floor, call upon God! And if you choose to pray aloud, right in the middle of life, your precious princess is likely to hear you and seek to do the same!

BRING YOUR CONCERNS

Your cares and concerns about your daughter are specific. God cares about every detail and every anxious thought. Are you worried about her current or future friends? struggling to teach her to obey? frustrated by her attitude? feeling that you failed lately in one or more areas of parenting? recognizing her need for something but not sure how to approach the topic with her? You can bring every one of these concerns to your heavenly King's throne of grace as many times as you need to. And each time you do, you can pray with an attitude of thanksgiving because He miraculously trades your anxious thoughts, cares, and concerns for His peace: **"Do not be anxious about anything, but in everything by prayer and supplication with thanksgiving let your requests be made known to God. And the peace of God, which surpasses all understanding, will guard your hearts and your minds in Christ Jesus"** (Philippians 4:6–7). Envision the peace that surpasses all understanding as though it is a guard standing post before your very heart and mind, protecting them from every anxious thought. This peace is yours in Christ Jesus!

ENLIST OTHERS

You and your family may be the only ones praying for your precious princess, but you don't have to go it alone. Enlist other prayer warriors who care about your girl. Ask those who may lack confidence in their own ability to pray for others; you will encourage them greatly as you entrust them with such an important task. I know this to be true because I was on the receiving end of such a request by another mom for the first time several years ago. Our young families had become acquainted in church, and I recognized this mother to be something special. Openly passionate about her faith in Christ and her desire to raise godly children, one day she boldly asked ME to pray for them, sharing specific and confidential petitions for her children and her family. I was humbled and honored that she asked me, and I wanted to be faithful to this privilege entrusted to me. God used this time to grow my prayer life to a place of greater consistency and trust.

"WHEN YOU LIE DOWN AND WHEN YOU RISE"

Remember the passage for parents in Deuteronomy 6? **"Teach them diligently to your children . . . talk of them when you sit in your house, and when you walk by the way, and when you lie down, and when you rise"** (v. 7). Did you catch the last part? Talking about the love of Christ and His Word includes teaching our princesses to begin and end their days in the Lord, teaching them to surround their day in the Word and in prayer—first thing and last thing.

How can we turn our day over to God in prayer and teach her to do the same? We could try waking her up with a one- or two-sentence prayer for God's protection and guidance through the day. We can lift her to the Lord as she's about to walk out the palace door or step out of the carriage to start the school day. For years, I prayed over my princess at the door; it gave me great comfort to entrust her and her brothers to the Lord, even as they witnessed my trust and dependence on God for guidance and received the blessing of being on the receiving end of "when you rise" prayers.

Bedtime prayer, either with family devotions or during tuck-in time, is the perfect way to send your princess off to sleep in her Savior's arms. What could be more comforting, whether she is three or thirteen? It can be the healing balm on her hard days and the place of security and safety on her scary days. It's a time to recall the events of the day, helping her hand them over to the Lord, and to rejoice over ALL days, whatever they may bring.

As I prayed with Courtney, I would often stroke her hair while I sat on the edge of her bed. Inevitably, she would have questions following our prayers, and often she would open up about her worries or fears or what went wrong that day. If her father or I had been upset with her, or vice versa, we were able to resolve it there. And then she would ask for a song (an amazing request from someone who's actually heard me sing!). "Someone Special" and "I Love You, Lord" were favorites in our special routine. "When you lie down" is your opportunity to give your princess one last peace-filled reminder that her heavenly Father is watching over her and protecting her; He loves her, and so do you. **"In peace I will both lie down and sleep; for You alone, O Lord, make me dwell in safety"** (Psalm 4:8).

FOR AND WITH YOUR PRINCESS

Model prayer as you teach it to your dear daughter. Pray openly and honestly. Let her hear you confess your sins and praise your Maker. Let her listen as you thank Him for the many blessings of the day and as you hold her up in prayer.

Prayer for and with your precious girl is not another task you complete and check off your good-mom to-do list. It's one of the most powerful things you can do for and with her, not because your words are impressive or powerful, but because you have a mighty God who hears and answers your prayers offered to Him in Jesus' name. Believe that the Lord pow-erfully works through her as she listens to your prayer and grows in the same trust that you model by taking everything to the Lord in prayer.

♥ How can you be purposeful and intentional about your prayers for and with your princess? You may already know her heart and her needs better than any other person. Make a prayer list or begin a prayer journal. Ask her what you can pray for. What are her current needs? concerns? joys? Consider how you can cover her future needs and concerns too: a spouse, education plans, career, and more.

♥ Pray for her continued growth in faith, that God would continue to work in her heart, transforming her in Christ's image (2 Corinthians 3:18); that she would grow in her desire to follow His will and imitate Him at every turn; and that she would look to His Word for guidance in all of life's decisions.

♥ When you do not know what to say or how to pray, when you're exhausted or overwhelmed or discouraged, wondering how you can pray for and with your princess, cling to these words and teach them to her: **"The Spirit helps us in our weakness. For we do not know what to pray for as we ought, but the Spirit Himself intercedes for us with groanings too deep for words"** (Romans 8:26). Ask the Spirit to guide your way!

PRAY THE SCRIPTURES

Pray the Scriptures for and with your daughter, inserting her name into them. I had the privilege of praying with other moms for my children during their elementary school years as part of a weekly moms' prayer group. The following are a few of my favorites, as I prayed them for each child. Perhaps they'll provide a great place for you to start:

"For this reason I bow my knees before the Father, from whom every family in heaven and on earth is named, that according to the riches of His glory He may grant you, _____, to be strengthened with power through His Spirit in your inner being, so that Christ may dwell in your hearts through faith—that you, _____, being rooted and grounded in love, may have strength to comprehend with all the saints what is the breadth and length and height and depth, and to know the love of Christ that surpasses knowledge, that you, _____, may be filled with all the fullness of God" (Ephesians 3:14–19).

"It is my prayer that your love may abound more and more, with knowledge and all discernment, so that you, _____, may approve what is excellent, and so be pure and blameless for the day of Christ, filled with the fruit of righteousness that comes through Jesus Christ, to the glory and praise of God" (Philippians 1:9–11).

"We have not ceased to pray for you, _____, asking that you may be filled with the knowledge of His will in all spiritual wisdom and understanding, so as to walk in a manner worthy of the Lord, fully pleasing to Him, bearing fruit in every good work and increasing in the knowledge of God" (Colossians 1:9–10).

GUIDE HER TO A LIFE OF PRAYER

Lead your growing girl to pray, helping her see the need for it and the power of God in and through it. Guide her into a life of prayer. The following are some ideas to help you along the way:

- From her earliest toddler years, you can teach her to stop and pray for others when she hears sirens or when she witnesses any other potentially scary situation.

- Encourage your growing girl, and praise her for her humble words given to God in prayer. No matter how long or short her prayer, it is a beautiful offering to Him.

- Teach her how she can "pray without ceasing," offering pop-up prayers in the middle of the day and developing an attitude of constant prayer and dependence on God.

- Pray for and with your daughter on the spot as a crisis or need arrives: when she walks through the door in tears, when you learn of another family's illness or accident, or when another person suddenly comes to mind.

- Develop a prayer habit for your family at regular times in your daily routine, such as mealtime, devotion time, and bedtime, if possible.

- Sing the doxology or a table prayer set to music, encouraging your girl to sing with no inhibitions as she offers praise and thanks to the Lord.

- Pray with her about big and small things, revealing that it all matters to God. He is a God of details and desires that we bring them all to Him.

💜 Encourage her to be honest and forthright in her prayers. God knows every hair on her head, so He surely knows everything on her heart. She can pray about anything, even those things that she can't talk to you about.

💜 Tell your princess that however her heavenly Father answers her prayers—yes, no, or wait—she can expect Him to change and grow her as a result of her prayers.

💜 Present her with a journal, and encourage her to record her prayers and others' prayer requests. Encourage her to look back to her past journal entries, recognizing God's provision and answers along the way.

Whatever her age, your princess already faces fears, worries, and concerns. Teach her to take each one to God in prayer. While she's still quite young, she'll begin to wonder about the future and dream of what she'll do, who she will meet, and even where she'll live. Talk to God with her concerning those thoughts and dreams. Whether or not she realizes it, your daughter is moving forward in preparation for the future, toward the plans that her Creator has for the pages of her life story that are yet to be read. As you remind her that her loving heavenly Father's eyes are always upon her, guide her to seek His will as she goes to Him in prayer for direction and discernment, to recognize the gifts He has given, and to use them to prepare herself for the path and the future that only He can see. He says to you and your daughter, **"I will instruct you and teach you in the way you should go; I will counsel you with My eye upon you"** (Psalm 32:8).

DON'T CONFORM—BE TRANSFORMED!

"Do not be conformed to this world, but be transformed by the renewal of your mind, that by testing you may discern what is the will of God, what is good and acceptable and perfect" (Romans 12:2). Help your dear daughter see her need to pray. Teach her the truth that she is not self-sufficient, as the world would have her believe, but very much reliant on the Lord and His grace for every page of her life story, on the good days and the not-so-good days. Remind her that when life is good and days are full of laughter and fun, it can be easy to forget to pray. By our own sin, the suggestions of the world around us, and the lies of the evil one, we begin to think that we're somehow operating in our own strength. Then the not-so-good days hit, and we're humbly reminded of our need for His power and His grace. Pray with your daughter that God would continue to renew your minds, enabling you to recognize your need for continual communication with your Savior, through the Word and in prayer.

I've heard unbelieving critics say that prayer is for the weak. While they're sadly off the mark, thinking that the believer who prays to God has taken the weak position of dependence upon someone outside of his or herself, what they say is also true, in a totally different sense. We can help our daughters recognize this form of religious persecution and teach them how to respond when they're the recipients of a verbal attack. A response could be, "You're right. I'm weak. I'm a weak sinner in need of an all-powerful God who sent His Son to die for my sins. I pray to the One whose power is made perfect in my weakness. And I'd like to pray for you too" (see 2 Corinthians 12:9). Some experts in the medical community recognize the power of prayer too. Extensive clinical studies have been done regarding the effects of prayer on health and healing. Mitchell Krucoff, MD, a cardiovascular specialist at Duke University School of Medicine in Durham, North Carolina, told Web MD, "All of these studies, all the reports, are remarkably consistent in suggesting the potential measurable health benefit associated with prayer." The results of the nearly 1,200 clinical studies also indicate that people who pray tend to lead healthier lives and get sick less often (webmd.com/balance/features/can-prayer-heal [02-02-15]). Despite the claims of unbelieving critics, there is evidence for the power of prayer, power that rests in the hands of the one true God, who hears and answers every prayer according to His will.

A WORD OF GRACE

How often do we fail to pray simply because we lack the faith? We've determined that it probably won't change the status quo. Or we've selfishly treated it like a magic wand. Or maybe we've minimalized the power of prayer by saying or thinking, "All we can do is pray." Whether we've struggled to see that prayer changes things or asked for selfish purposes (wanting an answer "waved" in our direction according to our desires) or thought it a lesser priority than some other action we can take, we've missed the mark. We've failed to see that we have a mighty God who hears our every prayer and answers in His perfect wisdom. When we come before Him, sorry for our lack of trust, our selfish desires, or our failure to make prayer a top priority, our heavenly Father, who **"knows what you need before you ask Him"** (Matthew 6:8) forgives us for Jesus' sake! He knows before we ask Him that we are in desperate need of His grace, and He supplies it richly.

Forgiven and filled with the Holy Spirit's power, we are able to see God working through our prayers; according to His will, He may change the status quo, change us, or both! He knows best. We no longer wish to have prayer "waved" our way according to our desires, but ask that He answer according to His will. We realize that prayer is not "all we can do" but one of the most important and life-changing things we can do for the recipient and for the sender (us). By God's amazing grace, our daughters will see us grow in faith as we grow in prayer, humbly admit our shortcomings and attempts at self-reliance, and reveal to our growing girls the dependence we have upon God, **"who richly provides us with everything to enjoy"** (1 Timothy 6:17).

SHOW AND TELL

1. I have found *ACTS* to be a helpful acronym when I pray. Maybe you'll find this or something similar that will guide you as you set aside time for prayer and as you seek to model it for your daughter. Give Him your *Adoration* or praise, for who He is and what He has done. Bring your *Confessions* of sin before Him, asking for His forgiveness. Pray with a heart full of *Thanksgiving* for His provision, protection, answered prayers, and more. Bring *Supplications* to Him, both requests of your own and on behalf of others.

2. What's one action you can take today and in the week ahead to be more intentional about becoming (or growing further as) the praying mom that your sweet princess needs you to be?

    Determine and schedule a specific time of day that you'll set aside for prayer.

✳ Create a prayer list, or begin a journal to include specific prayers for her; revisit this list or journal over time, and log the ways in which they've been answered.

✳ Enlist others to pray for your daughter; join with them for prayer when possible.

3. What can you teach your daughter today about prayer? Look to Jesus as the perfect role model; He made prayer a top priority. Check out Mark 1:35 together. Look to Jesus' words in Matthew 6:9–13, as He taught His disciples to pray. Pray the Lord's Prayer together and talk about the meaning of each petition.

4. Ask your daughter what specific things she'd like prayers for right now on this page of her life story. (Even if she's still very young, you can begin to ask her!) Let her see you write them down, then follow up with her on a regular basis to continue good communication about important matters. This will help both of you see how God is working through your prayers for her, even when His answers are not immediate or don't look quite how you or she had expected.

Chapter 6

Like Mother, Like Daughter—
Imitating the Queen's Qualities

> Therefore be imitators of God, as beloved children. And walk in
> love, as Christ loved us and gave Himself up for us. Ephesians 5:1–2

I'VE BECOME MY MOTHER

One year for Mother's Day, I gave my mom a humorous greeting card that said: "I'm always using the wisdom and advice you've given me, Mom . . . " The greeting continued inside: "Sometimes I even do it using your voice and mannerisms. I'm pretty good." Similarly, my sister gave me a mug that proclaimed, "I've become my mother." I may have rolled my eyes at these silly sentiments when I was younger, but now I find them endearing (and there's some truth in them too!). I'm humbled and blessed as I recognize that I have some of my mother's qualities. From the earliest chapters of my life story to the present pages, she has provided me with words of wisdom from God and solid advice of her own for daily living. And I can imitate her just like that without even realizing it: from her native dialect, to her favorite colloquialisms, to her nervous, energetic nature! Similarly, my daughter recently remarked that she's become much like me. Should I be surprised? (Probably not!)

Can you relate? How and why is it that we may "become our mothers" in some (or many) ways? Our mothers, the queens of our home palaces, are our earliest and often most influential role models, according to a 2015 article in WebMD. They are the nurturers with whom we spend a great deal of time during our formative years—and the ones we're most likely to imitate, because that's what children naturally do. Likewise, our daughters want to imitate us and our qualities even before they can express that desire in words. We begin to see glimpses of ourselves in them, not only in appearance, but especially through words and actions, beginning in the earliest chapters of their life stories. *That can be a scary thought, can't it?*

I like to think all of my words and actions are godly and positive, but I know I'm not a perfect parent. Far from it! I know all too well the areas where I struggle and the weaknesses that I'm afraid I'll pass on to my daughter. And I know I'm not alone. One mom shared with me the burden she feels when she hears biting sarcasm flow from the lips of her teenage girls, recognizing it as her own. Another mom winces when she hears her own snarky statements come from her five-year-old. Still another mom laments that some days she recognizes her own negative expressions of worry, anxiety, or anger in her girls. In our sinful human condition, we relate with these struggles and weaknesses. But as we confess them to our gracious God, we can trust that He will use our very struggles to help us see our need for His lead, His strength, and His guidance as we parent, recognizing that we cannot go it alone. My daughter doesn't have the perfect mother, but by God's grace, she has a forgiven one!

IMITATORS OF GOD

We want to make every word count, don't we? To consider every action and every choice we make as each relates to its potential influence on our little imitators. If they're watching our every move and mimicking our every word, would we desire any less than to imitate God? And again, by His grace, we can! **"Therefore be imitators of God, as beloved children. And walk in love, as Christ loved us and gave Himself up for us"** (Ephesians 5:1–2). Once again, God calls us His children—even beloved children—because we are! And children are the best imitators, aren't they? What does it look like to imitate our heavenly Father? The Bible tells us that imitating Him means we love others with the same kind of sacrificial love that Christ had for us when He went to the cross. That is the sacrificial love a mother has for her precious princess.

Imitating Christ, we walk in love, communicating that love openly and honestly with words: "I love you and I like you." Shower them sincerely, deliberately upon your daughter. Your words clearly communicate her great value and worth. As she drifts off to sleep, as she wakes up, and as she leaves for school; as she rejoices in her victories and cries in her defeats. You can be there for her, saying, "I love you and I like you. Always. I love you not because of anything you have done or not done. I love you simply because you are my child. And though I may not like your behavior sometimes, I like YOU!"

Our Father God's spoken words of love for us reveal that His love is not contingent upon our behavior either. In fact, He loves us in spite of and in the midst of our sinful behavior. He shares His great love for us in words (all across His Word!) and in the greatest demonstration of love in all history. It's at the very heart of HIS STORY: **"But God shows His love for us in that while we were still sinners, Christ died for us"** (Romans 5:8). And His love for us makes it possible for us, in turn, to love our children, both with our spoken words of love to them and by our demonstration of it.

WORDS WORTHY OF IMITATION

A friend of mine recalls a Walgreens shopping adventure with her four children in tow. It was a special excursion, complete with a trip to the toy aisle, where each child got to select something to purchase with hard-earned "Kids in Charge Day" money. After lots of time in the toy aisle helping each child choose just the right toy (and attempting to keep her youngest daughter from removing every item from the shelves), she made it to the checkout lane with each child possessing a special find, a handful of cash, and lots of energy. My frazzled friend told me the thought had crossed her mind, *Oh, why did we come? What a circus!* The line of shoppers grew behind them as each child used his or her own money to pay, and all the while, the littlest one was trying to crawl out of the cart. My friend explained, "The kind lady checking us out said, 'You are a good Mom,' and I responded, 'Thank you, that is so kind of you to say,' but I was not feeling like this was one of my top Mommy moments! From behind me, I heard a voice say, 'You are.' It was my oldest daughter, Macey. I didn't realize she was even paying attention to our conversation. That made it all worth it. With those two words, she made my world right. The weight of those two words. It reminded me of the weight of my words and how I can also make their world right with just a simple statement."

Macey observed her mom's every move long before their trip to the store. Sometimes, all we focus on is our current struggle. But maybe our sweet daughters see much more of the picture. Guess what? You're a good mom too! And your words and actions, guided by God's Word, can be worthy of imitation. How can you "make their world right" with your words? **"Let no corrupting talk come out of your mouths, but only such as is good for building up, as fits the occasion, that it may give grace to those who hear"** (Ephesians 4:29).

Let's take a close look, pondering each piece of this verse as it relates to our words and their impact upon our daughters' world:

💜 **NO CORRUPTING TALK**– Corrupting talk comes in many forms, and God's Word speaks very clearly against every one of them. Colossians 3:8 tells us we must get rid of **"obscene talk."** Ephesians 5:4 says, **"Let there be no filthiness nor foolish talk nor crude joking, which are out of place, but instead let there be thanksgiving."** Foul language, crude jokes, and the like are never appropriate. Why waste words that can corrupt our character and damage our witness to our daughters? Why waste words that are clearly "out of place" when our mouths can be used instead for good, for thanksgiving? The very name of the Lord is corrupted when spoken in vain, and as one of His Ten Commandments proclaims: **"You shall not take the name of the LORD your God in vain, for the Lord will not hold him guiltless who takes His name in vain"** (Exodus 20:7).

Until recently, I didn't realize the impact that the absence or presence of these words had on Courtney while she was growing up. She said, "When I first heard parents swear, I was shocked. For a long, long time, I thought it was totally taboo. Now I'm not as offended, but I still don't want to swear. I appreciated that you didn't. From your example, I know a person can express herself without having to use naughty words or take God's name in vain. I just wish you had told me what some of the words and innuendos were, so I would have been better prepared when I was suddenly surrounded by them in high school." Although I'd protected my daughter as much as I could from corrupting talk, I recognize now that she needed preparation, as well as protection, since obscene talk is commonplace in our world. I'd taught my daughter the simple phrase "garbage in—garbage out" to remind her not to even listen to verbal refuse so she wouldn't be tempted to imitate it. But at school, at the mall, and in other situations, it is impossible to avoid. Praise God for the discernment He gave her to determine which kind of talk to imitate.

Have you witnessed a woman routinely speaking a certain sweet way while chatting with others, only to speak another way entirely with her children? While it's not my place or yours to judge that mom for this kind of corrupting talk, perhaps one reason we inwardly cringe is that we've seen it in ourselves as well. While recognizing my misplaced judgment and seeking God's forgiveness for my critical thoughts, I've also prayed that God would enable me to use observations like this for the good of my own family as I examine my own speech and determine, with God's help, to choose differently, to guard my tongue in every conversation, speaking with grace and respect regardless of the audience. **"Set a guard, O Lord, over my mouth"** (Psalm 141:3).

What will your princess overhear you say to others over the phone, in the palace, and around the kingdom? Pay attention to your conversation with other adults. Is gossip involved? Have corrupting words or remarks tumbled from your mouth, revealing negative attitudes or even hate toward others? Has she heard you betray a confidence? **"With [the tongue] we bless our Lord and Father, and with it we curse people who are made in the likeness of God. From the same mouth come blessing and cursing. My brothers, these things ought not to be so"** (James 3:9–10). You and I are guilty of cursing people in some manner or another, and we desperately need God's grace and forgiveness. We also need His help to change our hearts regarding our words and our attitudes against others. Ask God to guide you away from every form of corrupting talk, from crude jokes and verbal garbage to hurtful, negative words lashed out at or about others. He will lead you, instead, to words that build up!

❤ **GOOD FOR BUILDING UP–** Oh, that our words would always build up our growing girls! Even when it appears that she's not listening or when you don't think you're actually being heard, know that your words do have impact. As you seek God's lead, trust that He is at work through you and that the godly wisdom you impart will surface in her life when it's most needed. From the beginning, she has heard you; she has learned that she can trust your words to be true. So when you express sincere words of affirmation for a job well done, an earnest effort, or a valiant attempt, she is encouraged and resolves to keep trying, also trusting God's work in her, by your witness. She is strengthened to live up to her God-given potential, and she is also fortified to withstand the verbal assaults that may come from peers or critical adults.

Let's take this a step further: Every time your daughter hears you building up someone else, she is further encouraged, recognizing that your sincere words are giving grace to someone else too! **"Therefore encourage one another and build one another up, just as you are doing"** (1 Thessalonians 5:11). As you place others and their needs ahead of your own, you model for your princess to go and do likewise.

♥ **FITTING FOR THE OCCASION–** Our words, carefully chosen, may build up our girls on every occasion, in every situation. And one such occasion involves discipline and instruction. **"Fathers [and mothers], do not provoke your children to anger, but bring them up in the discipline and instruction of the Lord"** (Ephesians 6:4). Our words of discipline, when shared out of love and for our dear daughters' good, are some of the most effective and endearing we can share. Gently teach right from wrong, explaining why rules are given for their good, sharing God's truth as the guide for this instruction. While we're not to "provoke [them] to anger," that doesn't mean we avoid difficult conversations that include redirection, correction, or consequences. But as we have these critical conversations, we speak carefully and intentionally with a demeanor that is kind, helpful, and shows that we desire the best for her.

My friend Nicole told me about a fitting occasion for a few special building-up words with her little girl, right in the middle of redirection. Her strong-willed three-year-old, Anisten, had what you might call a short fuse. For example, if she couldn't get her shoe on, she would immediately be on her back, crying loudly. Unlike Nicole's other children when they were this age, Anisten could not be distracted from her tantrum. Then, Nicole tried something different. She shared, "As Anisten was having a little fit, I whispered, 'I love you Anisten.' She stopped and responded in a grumpy, pouty voice, 'I love you too, Mommy.' With a smile, she then repeated it in her sweet little voice. I did this throughout the week, whispering an 'I love you' in the midst of every tantrum, and it stopped every one. And the last time she was crying and upset, I didn't even have to say a word! I just looked at her; she stopped crying, smiled, and said, 'I love you, Mommy.'" Anisten mimicked her mommy's gentle response, receiving not only redirection but also the reminder of her mother's love through the best building-up words a girl could hear. The next time we're at our worst, maybe we can remember to tell God "I love You" in response to His tender love for us.

❤ GIVING GRACE TO THOSE WHO HEAR– I was asked to speak at a retreat specifically for moms. I recall feeling discouraged and distracted as I prepared to lead because I felt so unworthy of encouraging other Christian moms in their task of raising royalty. I'd been focused instead on some recent blunders with my own Kingdom kids, and I even wondered if I was having a lasting positive impact upon them. The retreat leader had secretly asked our husbands to write and send letters that would be read at the end of our getaway event. My husband's words gave grace to me when I most needed it. In part, this is what he wrote:

"You bring such joy to our family, yet so often you are too close to notice it. I see it in our kids. They reflect your joy when we least expect it: when they ask you to 'tell a story from when you were a kid,' when Courtney gets a piano piece just right and laughs when you gently remind her that she told you, 'I'll NEVER get it right.' They reflect your joy at bedtime when they hear the devotions and give their wonderful prayers. The only reason they reflect your joy and love is because of who you reflect to them. They see Christ reflected in you and through you. Sure, they see the warts sometimes, but they won't remember them; they will remember [and imitate] Christ's joy flowing from you."

Do you sometimes see only the warts and fail to recognize the positive impact of your words upon your precious princess? Trust that as Christ works in your life, He empowers you to be able to imitate Him and she'll see His joy flowing from you!

As your words build up, giving grace to those who hear them, consider who may *overhear* them too! Consider that other moms, who may be in the midst of their own trying times, may hear you speak words that build up others, and they will emulate you! It's quite possible that your daughter has also overheard uplifting words that you've shared with others about her. When she overhears you, she will recognize your support and love to be unconditional and your praise to be genuine.

Your words reveal the Lord's grace and work in your life. Tell your daughter what He has done for you; share specific details, including everything from answered prayers to the ways and places that you've witnessed His miraculous power at work, in and through you and others! And yes, just as the hymn says, "I love to tell the story, . . . To tell the old, old story Of Jesus and His love"! Tell her, again and again, the story of salvation. Share your favorite passages and your go-to verses in difficult times. **"We will not hide them from their children, but tell to the coming generation the glorious deeds of the Lord, and His might, and the wonders that He has done"** (Psalm 78:4). As discussed previously, you have the privilege of sharing His Words of grace, giving *her* grace as you do.

ACTIONS SPEAK LOUDER

As we seek to imitate God, we live a life of love, in words *and* in actions. **"Little children, let us not love in word or talk but in deed and in truth"** (1 John 3:18). You've probably heard it said that actions speak louder than words. What are your actions shouting to her? Are they filled with God-imitating love?

Several years ago, as I was preparing to speak before a group of Christian moms with encouragement for their vocation, my then nine-year-old advised me, "Mom, I think you should tell them it's more about what you do than what you say." While your words of love are vitally important, they may be questioned or doubted if your walk doesn't match your talk. And your daughter's actions will likely mimic yours.

♥ **MARRIAGE**—With God's help, commit to giving this number-one earthly relationship the priority it needs. Love him, honor his roles as husband, father, and king of the palace. Respect his authority (Ephesians 5:33), and speak with the same kindness you'd like to receive from him. Set aside time for communication as a couple apart from your princess and the entire royal family. Come to an agreement on parenting matters, and present a united plan for decisions and discipline regarding your children. Seek forgiveness and offer it. Your daughter doesn't need to see a seemingly-perfect marriage; that would be artificial and possibly set her up for unrealistic expectations. What she needs to see is genuine love, trust, and forgiveness. This witness is invaluable to your daughter's well-being, both now and as she faces the future, looking to her parents for an example that she can emulate.

If you are struggling in your marriage, seek the help of your pastor or a Christian counselor. By God's grace, you can act with integrity toward your husband, even when it's difficult. You can still teach your daughter what a healthy marriage can look like, even if your marriage is going through a tough time—and even if you're a single mom. Connect with families who provide positive examples for your impressionable girl. Ask a trusted friend to help you mentor your daughter in this area, especially as she reaches the age where she may begin to date. Study together what God's Word says about marriage and relationships. With the assistance of a mentor or pastor, plan what you will say to your daughter about the circumstances of your single life. Your story can be a powerful testimony of God's grace in Christ and His ability to redeem every difficult or damaging situation.

♥ **WORK ETHIC**—Your life speaks loudly as you reveal your work ethic day after day. Give your best as you work wholeheartedly and cheerfully in your vocations, whether inside the palace, beyond the palace gates, or both. **"Whatever you do, work heartily, as for the Lord and not for men"** (Colossians 3:23). With a dedication to excellence, be thankful for meaningful work, whatever your vocation, even when the meaning of it may not seem full to you. Let her see that you and your husband are grateful for an honest day's work, trusting that God will use it to impact someone, even if it's unseen by you.

I'm reminded of a fairy-tale princess with a great attitude and work ethic. Snow White even sang as she completed menial labor, cleaning up after others while facing piles of dishes and the dwarves' dirty cottage. (Sound familiar?!) Oh, for a heart to "whistle while we work!" We ask that God would **"teach us to number our days that we may get a heart of wisdom"** from Him (Psalm 90:12). How can we make the most of every moment, that we may grow to have that heart of wisdom? The dwarves' lives were changed forever by their surprise guest, and it began with her heart of service for them. Your life speaks volumes to your real-life princess as she sees your work ethic and your heart for others.

ADVERSITY—Your daughter receives her first cues in how to handle adversity, conflict, fear, failure, rejection, discouragement, and the like from what she sees in you. From the small daily crises to the largest blows, every adversity provides the opportunity for us to live out what we try to teach, and we lean into God's strong arms to do that in a healthy manner, relying on His grace for each time that we fail. Consider before adversity strikes how you'll handle it when it does: will you react rashly or respond prayerfully and patiently? The action you choose inadvertently gives your princess permission to follow and do likewise. Let her know that you take each difficult situation to Christ. She will see that you cling to the One who holds you up in tough times and learn that a healthy response in difficult times is possible not because you possess the strength or have the answer in every situation, but because you cling to the One who does!

A friend shared with me that she went to the grocery store one day and let her grade-school-aged girls stay home alone. She said, "Wouldn't you know that a severe thunderstorm warning occurred in the brief time I was gone? Well, I hurried home to find them huddled in the basement with their Bibles in hand. Usually, when a storm occurs and we need to go to the basement, I grab a Bible. I didn't realize that they had picked up on that!" My friend's precious girls were clinging to God's Word in more ways than one, imitating their mother's faith-filled actions as they did.

INTEGRITY—I've heard it said that integrity is who we are when we don't think anyone is watching. Your actions are a result of the morals, values, and integrity you possess, and they deeply impact your children, who witness you in public places and in the privacy of your home. Do you alert the store clerk when an error is made in your favor? Are your entertainment choices in line with what you claim them to be? Do you obey the laws of the land when no one will notice either way?

We all face many "opportunities" that are really temptations in disguise. Your daughter does too, and she'll be so much more likely to see them for what they are and run in the opposite direction if she has seen you do the same. Seek God's strength and clear guidance for yourself and for your daughter to walk in your integrity. **"The righteous who walks in [her] integrity—blessed are [her] children after [her]!"** (Proverbs 20:7).

When Courtney was younger, I was faced with a moral decision involving her and some of her peers. I had the choice between going with the flow and keeping my mouth shut, thereby saving potential ridicule for both of us, or courageously speaking out, as I believed the Lord was leading and empowering me to do. I chose the latter, and although I suffered a few repercussions from others, I gained further respect from my daughter. Later, she wrote a note to me that included these words: "I really admire the strong faith that you have and how you stand true to your morals even when everyone around you doesn't. That inspires me so much, and I want to be like you." Looking back, I remembered that my mother had chosen likewise in similar situations during my growing-up years. She walked in integrity, even when it wasn't the popular thing to do, and I was blessed as a result. I believe that my daughter, by God's grace, will someday do the same.

"JUST LIKE YOU"

"Hear, my [child], your father's instruction, and forsake not your mother's teaching" (Proverbs 1:8). About six years ago, my friend Elizabeth began a weekly routine that continues today. She calls it her "appointment with God at Starbucks," where she meets with God every Sunday morning before worship. "I enjoy hot chocolate, but even more, I enjoy my time with God as I pray and reflect on my life, read Scripture, and write devotions. I look forward to it every week and have hardly missed an appointment." After her daughter began college, Elizabeth would ask periodically if she was taking time to read the Bible and spend time with God. For a while, the answer was no. Her daughter was involved with many activities and hadn't gotten into a routine yet. In her second semester, she wrote her mother a letter telling her how she started going to a coffee shop every Thursday morning before class to spend time with God. She closed with the words "Just like you do, Mom."

We pray, by God's work in our lives, that our loving witness to our girls and to everyone else would be the same as that of the apostle Paul, who said, **"Be imitators of me, as I am of Christ"** (1 Corinthians 11:1).

DON'T CONFORM—BE TRANSFORMED!

It's all too easy to imitate the ways of the world. How often do we hear our children mimicking the words of a commercial, the lyrics to a song, the questionable attitudes and actions of an envied peer or pop star, the popular catchphrase of the day? And don't we easily fall into the same imitating habits? As we keep an attentive ear and a watchful eye on the words, actions, and attitudes that enter our home, we can remind our impressionable daughters of God's safe-guarding words from Romans 12:2: **"Do not be conformed to this world, but be transformed by the renewal of your mind, that by testing you may discern what is the will of God, what is good and acceptable and perfect."** Are the easily-imitated words, lyrics, attitudes, and actions harmless and merely a passing fad, or can they be corrupting? Seize opportunities to talk to your daughter about the subtle ways we succumb to cultural examples. Use teachable moments to point out where she may be conforming to the world by imitation or by believing the messages before her at school, on the Internet, in media, and in virtually every aspect of life today.

God continually works transformation in you, that you may be a little imitator of Christ. ("Little Christ" is the very definition of *Christian*!) And by your imitation, your dear daughter can witness God's **"good and acceptable and perfect"** will through you, as you help her discern what's worth imitating!

A WORD OF GRACE

Some days, we may not be able to see that our princesses have learned anything good from us; it may seem that they have not heard our many words or paid attention to the example we've sought to show. Are we making a difference on the pages and chapters of their life stories? We teach something and think that they "get" it. Then they go right back to their former ways, and we worry that they haven't learned by our example or listened to a thing we've said. We wish it were as simple as (a) say and do this, and (b) expect this result from our daughters. (We all want instant gratification, right?) Instead, they may be resistant to our lead and stubbornly wish to go their own way. We can relate! We want individuality. We want to blaze our own trails. At the same time, we're all in need of God's grace, freely given to us by faith in Christ.

Continue to gently redirect and discipline your growing girl, guiding her by God's grace and according to His Word. As you do, bear in mind that while your growing princess may be much like you and will imitate you in some ways, she is also her own unique person. And by God's design, she may do some things differently than you do. Don't expect or even strive for a carbon copy of yourself. Embrace her unique bent and different way of learning as she, too, grows in the image of Christ, with the ability to imitate Him for others to see.

Praise God for His grace that covers you in Christ Jesus and for the work of the Holy Spirit in your life, giving you the ability to talk the talk and walk the walk and to be transparent about your faith and desire to share it with your growing girl in real and meaningful ways, as your life story overlaps with hers.

SHOW AND TELL

1. Reflect on ways your daughter is similar to you. How are you alike in appearance? in personality? in your actions and responses? How are you different? What qualities do you possess that you would most like to see your daughter imitate?

2. Women are known for our quantity of words. Stereotyp- ically, at least, we have more to share than men do on a given day. And our little imitators are likely to follow suit. Consider God's warning: **"When words are many, transgression is not lacking, but whoever restrains his lips is prudent"** (Proverbs 10:19). What might help you be more mindful of every word? Prayerfully consider and discuss.

3. Begin today or continue to talk with transparency, humility, and honesty with your daughter. Not only will you both benefit from your strong communication, but you're also showing her that she can imitate you and do the same. Welcome her words and listen attentively when she comes to you with a difficult or sensitive situation. Help her talk through options, always pointing her to God's Word; together, ask Him to guide her.

4. We give our daughters many good gifts by our words and our actions, but perhaps the greatest is the gift of our daily witness for Christ in our walk with Him and as we seek to imitate Him. How would you like your example to speak to her? What would you like her watching eyes to see?

Chapter 7

Making Appearances—
A Princess's True Beauty

Beholding as in a mirror the glory of the Lord, [we] are being transformed into the same image from glory to glory, just as by the Spirit of the Lord. 2 Corinthians 3:18 (NKJV)

MIRROR, MIRROR

"*Mirror, mirror on the wall, who's the fairest one of all?*" The evil queen in the classic fairy tale, Snow White, was consumed with her own beauty. And conveniently enough, she had a magic mirror at her disposal. She was so obsessed with her appearance that she routinely appeared before her magic mirror, incessantly asking it the same question just to appease herself that she remained the most beautiful. The queen had chosen to define herself by her outward beauty, or "fairness," so she was enraged when the mirror informed her that there was someone else who surpassed her as the fairest in the kingdom: Snow White. The queen did not understand that the mirror was referring to much more than a mere outward appearance. She had dressed the fair princess in rags, as a vain and jealous attempt to conceal the young woman's lovely appearance, but Snow White's inner beauty shone through. In fact, the mirror reported that rags could not hide her *gentle grace*, the beauty within.

What would you ask if you could make an appearance before a magic mirror? Would your insecurities or your vanity lead you to ask questions about your outward image: *Am I beautiful? Am I the best? Am I the fairest one of all?* (Depending upon your daughter's current age, you might want to ask her the same questions, also drawing from analogies across this chapter as you discuss a princess's true beauty together!)

We enter dangerous territory if our thoughts concerning our appearance are centered on acquiring or maintaining physical beauty and filling ourselves with self-centered pride when we are recognized for it. Soon, we may find ourselves measuring our value by our outward appearance and comparing ourselves to others, wondering how we measure up against them. Before long, we're in danger of becoming jealous and judgmental. The Lord warns us, **"For where jealousy and selfish ambition exist, there will be disorder and every vile practice"** (James 3:16). Yet much of the world equates beauty with worth. Some sociologists have conducted studies about human behavior based on physical appearance. Millions of dollars are spent every year on cosmetics, cosmetic surgery, and media dedicated to beauty. So it's no wonder that we, too, are easily ensnared by dangerous thinking. Another woman walks by us and we think, *I'll never look that good.* Or maybe we think, *I look better than* her, *don't I?* And all too easily, our daughters learn to do the same. How does your daughter think she compares as she makes an appearance before others?

MAKING AN APPEARANCE BEFORE OTHERS –COMPARISONS

Making an appearance before her peers can feel like a test for a growing girl, especially as she grades herself next to others. Does she pass? Is she at the top of the class or the bottom? Where does she fit in? Gently warn your princess that when she compares herself to another, she's setting herself up for disappointment or disillusionment. If she feels that she falls short in appearance, apparel, or personality, she'll be disappointed in herself and suffer from a bad case of discontentment and insecurity. And if she feels that she has outdone another in any of these areas, she'll be disillusioned by selfish pride.

Likewise, as queen of your palace, you must not be tempted to compare yourself to another queen or to compare your past self with your present. Putting down another mother so you'll *appear* better by comparison isn't going to improve your quality of mothering—or your attitude, for that matter. Along the same lines, don't be tempted to compare your princess to someone else's, in physical appearance or in any other way. "She looks so nice. Why can't you be more like her? She *appears* to behave better than you too!"

Small comparisons may seem harmless, but if we and our daughters allow them to grow disproportionately, if we long for someone's "perfect" appearance or enviable personality, we've predetermined that we don't measure up and that we appear *less-than* to the rest of the world too. Remember that outward appearance provides a very limited view—one that can be deceptive.

The media has perfected the art of unfair comparisons. Magazines show airbrushed images of underweight models, and Hollywood portrays actresses as flawless in appearance, creating unrealistic ideals and unattainable so-called perfection. You and I may see through the façade for the artificial and unhealthy images that they are, but an impressionable preteen or teenage girl can see them as something to be desired, even envied, especially when her peers are attempting to emulate them. Again, gently warn your daughter of the dangers of unfair, unrealistic comparisons. Take the opportunity to view media together, teaching her how to discern between reality and make-believe, seeking God's wisdom as you do.

MAKING APPEARANCES ON SOCIAL MEDIA

Much like other media, the Internet, and specifically social media, creates places for unfair comparison traps. Smartphone technology makes it possible to access social media sites anytime and anywhere. Why is this significant? The limited view your sweet princess receives of others via social media is often skewed. Its impact is unique because it can be very personal, especially when the images and comments hit close to home and have been shared for the world to see. As friends share flattering photos and make enviable remarks, they may give the false impression that everything in their world is ideal. They may be making an appearance before their peers, attempting to build themselves up, to appear a certain way. The result? Your poor princess may end up resenting or feeling inferior to her friends, whose goal may not have been to intentionally hurt anyone, but merely to look good to others. In other cases, friends may share suggestive images or inappropriate content to seek negative attention and end up causing even further hurt as a result.

Research reveals a direct correlation between time spent on social media and negative feelings of self-worth, especially among growing girls who often struggle with confusion and uncertainty regarding their changing appearance, acceptance by peers, and very identity. Researchers from the School of Psychology at Flinders University in Australia surveyed more than one thousand adolescent girls. Dr. Amy Slater reported, "Our findings demonstrate a worrying correlation between excessive media use, particularly social media and the Internet, and lower self-esteem, body-esteem and sense of identity and higher depression" (medicaldaily.com/internet-lowers-self-esteme-teen-girls [02-03-15]).

Adults are not immune to its effects either. Many a mom has commiserated with me over another friend's attractive photos, impressive posts, and original food or craft creations. While they could inspire us, we're often envious instead. We fall into similarly deceptive comparison traps. In Galatians 5:26, the apostle Paul warns us, **"Let us not become conceited, provoking one another, envying one another."**

[On a personal note, I fall headlong into comparison traps because I think entirely too much *of* myself and *about* myself; otherwise, I wouldn't find myself stuck in the trap to begin with. I can blame social media for promoting a focus on self, but in my sin, I am predisposed to it already. As God lifts me out of my stuck place, enabling me to be others-focused, I can be glad for them and maybe even inspired as a result. I continue to take this struggle to the Lord in repentance and take what I'm learning to my daughter!]

I'm not advocating a ban of social media for us or our girls (once we've determined that they are old enough to make use of it). Many excellent Internet-driven tools for connectivity, conversation, and education have the potential to powerfully and positively impact us when we use them with discretion and with our eyes wide open to the potential deception and harm that can be found in them.

You have the opportunity to let social media be a great teaching tool for your daughter. Be the mom. Set limits and explain them clearly; define appropriate and inappropriate use; alert her to the very real dangers that exist. Don't mince words. If you've determined that she is ready for social media, then she must also be ready to understand the inherent dangers: Internet pornography, sexual innuendos, crude language, and other vices exist across cyberspace. Help safeguard her by providing ample information and clear-cut guidelines, all for her protection, so that she, too, has her eyes wide open. Pray for and with her, asking God to guard her heart and guard her eyes: **"Turn my eyes from looking at worthless things; and give me life in Your ways"** (Psalm 119:37). Establish a level of care and trust so she knows she can approach you with concerns and every possible scenario that may appear before her.

My daughter uses social media the way many young women her age do. She enjoys chatting and reconnecting with friends, sharing occasional photos of herself and others, pinning intriguing ideas, and sharing links to music videos and Christian articles. While Courtney has learned to use social media for helpful information and fun connections, she occasionally gets drawn into the comparison trap and admitted recently the frustrations she'd been facing concerning body image. "I know I could be more fit. And it doesn't help when I see pictures of girls with perfect abs on Pinterest. I think, 'If I do these exercises, I'll look like that . . . yeah, right. I'd have to spend *all* my time doing that!' It can become a source of guilt and comparison, so maybe I should just unfollow fitness boards. But then I go to other social media sites, and I see people I know posting pictures of their abs—and they look that good too! (Sigh)."

Your daughter is making an appearance before her peers when she sports her first smartphone, when she arrives on social media for the first time, sets up her first Facebook page or Instagram account, and *every* time she texts, posts, pins, or tweets (or whatever term the latest social media uses to define sharing something across cyberspace!). What kind of appearance will she want to portray? Help her to think carefully about the image she wishes to project, about how she wants to represent herself publicly. Encourage her as you remind her of her true identity as a godly girl. The image she projects doesn't have to try to impress because she is made in the image of God. Being transformed into Christ's likeness, her every appearance before others can be a reflection of Him by her character (2 Corinthians 3:18) as she chooses to reveal it, with God's help. What an opportunity! As she shares images of herself, words, interests, video clips, and more, she is free to express her unique identity as a chosen princess of His Majesty, the King.

MAKING AN APPEARANCE BEFORE THE LORD

As we continue to consider appearance, let's jump back to the classic Snow White tale and its princess. The mirror described the fair maiden as "white as snow." Was it referring to her outward appearance? Superficially, yes, but on a much deeper level, the mirror spoke of Snow White's inner qualities, her purity and her *gentle grace*. These characteristics defined the princess so well that she was named for them.

How does God define you? How does He define your daughter? When either of you make an appearance before the Lord, what does He see?

When the Lord looks upon you and your precious princess, He declares that you, too, are snow white! It's true. **"Though your sins are like scarlet, they shall be as white as snow"** (Isaiah 1:18). Although we are all stained by our sin, God's forgiveness in Christ cleanses us completely. Jesus' blood shed for us at the cross miraculously, fully, and freely purifies us. Once impure and tainted by our own vain and jealous thoughts, words, and actions, we are washed clean and purified in Christ. Daily, we remember our Baptism, receiving the reassurance that our sins are forgiven in Christ Jesus. We appear before God white as snow, covered in Christ.

So let's revisit again my earlier question. Pose it to yourself and to your daughter: *What would you ask if you could make an appearance before the proverbial magic mirror?* Maybe the questions you would ask run much deeper than those about physical appearance. *Am I loved? Am I valued?* The answer is a resounding YES! (And you don't need a make-believe magic mirror to tell you this. You'll find the answer in the very *real Word of God*.) Neither value nor true beauty is found in the facade. Your value is found in your true identity in Christ; it's found in your name: *child of God* (1 John 3:1). You are loved by Him; you are rescued from sin. You are so valuable because you are chosen and precious in His sight (1 Peter 2:4).

MAKEOVER

During my husband's seminary years, shortly after we had arrived at his vicarage assignment where he would train under a pastor, I attended the Saturday evening service with the children to hear my husband preach. But I had a cold. The virus had left me without a voice and without the will to even put on makeup. I wrote in my journal that "I felt kind of slimy, being sick and all!" I was hoping to slip in and out of service quietly and unnoticed with the children in tow. Wouldn't you know, a sweet couple seated behind us tapped my shoulder following the service and introduced themselves. Then the woman took a good look at me and tenderly said, "I would love to come to your home and give you a make-over." She even offered to purchase cosmetics for me. At first I thought that her generosity was linked to my husband's humble position and her desire to help his family in whatever way she could. But then I was overcome with thoughts of how unattractive I must appear. I knew the illness had left me pale, but I think the conversation caused me to grow even paler. And I sported an acne breakout to boot! I didn't know how to respond and could barely speak anyway, so I merely tried to be polite and receptive without acting thrilled at the prospect of a makeover.

Later, I wrote in my journal, "I try not to be vain about my appearance, but I am trying to step out with a good first impression and a polished appearance (not fancy, just present-able). And the first time I look truly sick, I get approached about a makeover!" A few days later, after my voice had returned, eight-year-old Courtney overheard me lamenting my story to her father, sharing the conversation as well as my feelings of insecurity over my appearance. She marched into the room and announced candidly, "Mom, I think you look better without makeup." She saw true beauty shining through the acne and the illness.

My daughter reminded me, through her straightforward words, of a truth I'd already been trying to teach her. Our beauty has less to do with the face we see in the mirror and a whole lot more to do with the countenance that reveals what's in our hearts. **"A glad heart makes a cheerful face, but by sorrow of heart the spirit is crushed"** (Proverbs 15:13).

What does your daughter's reflection really reveal? What's going on inside?

★ The countenance, the broad smile unique to her that reveals inner joy in Christ—with or without dimples and revealing all her teeth or just a few!

★ The compassionate glance that she gives when she looks on someone in need.

★ The look of love she openly shares with those closest to her.

★ The clenched jaw of anger, as she witnesses injustice and hate in her world.

★ The eyes wide with surprise or leaky from sadness and sorrow.

Eventually, my daughter began to experiment with makeup. At the end of middle school, she began to care about putting more effort into her appearance. My goal was to guide and encourage her as she made good choices regarding hygiene, self-care, and a healthy attention to her appearance. I hoped that my example was one that she would emulate as I sought not to be vain about my appearance or give too much attention to it, but to attempt to step out with a polished appearance.

Fast-forwarding nine years from the makeover offer, I stood in front of the bathroom mirror, applying makeup alongside my daughter and her friend Journey. "Age-Defying," Journey read out loud from my makeup bottle's label. "So how's that workin' for ya, Mrs. Burma?" Journey continued in a teasing tone.

Not missing a beat, I stroked my cheek while replying jokingly, "Beautifully! Why, I look one year younger every day that I apply it. Right now, I'm at age 25. Can't you tell?"

"Uh, yeah . . . right. Sure," she laughed, along with 17-year-old Courtney, who rolled her eyes at my ridiculous response.

A PRINCESS'S TRUE BEAUTY

When we gaze into a mirror, what else does our reflection reveal about beauty—TRUE beauty? Is it impacted by the makeup we put on (or don't put on, as the case may be)? Do we need a makeover? Or is there something incomparably better that we "put on," only by God's power at work in us? Can we put on inner character qualities that reveal true beauty and gentle grace?

> **"Put on then, as God's chosen ones, holy and beloved, compassionate hearts, kindness, humility, meekness, and patience, bearing with one another**

and, if one has a complaint against another, forgiving each other; as the Lord has forgiven you, so you also must forgive. And above all these put on love, which binds everything together in perfect harmony." (Colossians 3:12–14)

The question we can ask as we look into our mirrors each day (and as we lovingly lead our daughters to do the same) is simply, "How and where can I reflect Your image today, Jesus?" HE is the fairest one of all! He has a perfectly compassionate heart; He is completely kind, humble, meek, and patient; He fully and freely forgives; and He IS love!

And you and your precious princess are being remade in His likeness (Ephesians 4:24). He is performing a real makeover in you. **"Beholding as in a mirror the glory of the Lord, [we] are being transformed into the same image from glory to glory, just as by the Spirit of the Lord"** (2 Corinthians 3:18 NKJV).

MODESTY IN APPEARANCE

Chosen by God, made holy in Christ, and in the process of being transformed in His image, we represent Christ to the World. We *make an appearance* before our daughters and everyone else through our outward expression of the inner qualities He is growing in us, as He performs an inner makeover incomparably more impactful than any makeup we may or may not put on. Knowing this, we need to consider if our choices in clothing, as well as makeup, complement or hinder our witness as we represent Christ.

What message do we communicate in our manner of dress, especially to our impressionable daughters? If we desire to teach them to dress modestly, we must do more than merely talk about it; we must model it first. As we set examples for our princesses, we must not feel compelled to dress just like their generation in an attempt to be the coolest mom on the block. I'm not implying that we should dress like our grand-mothers, but we must be mindful of the message we convey every time we step out of our dressing room or out the door of the palace. We can choose fashions that are tasteful yet modest, while still stylish and even fun.

Teach your daughter what modesty means as you guide her to choose attractive clothing that includes both colors that com-plement her eyes and skin tone and styles that fit her well. Find a balance of tasteful and trendy. The fashion industry often likes to create miniature versions of women's styles for little girls, and sometimes it can be difficult to find appro-priate and modest styles of clothing even for a five-year-old. According to a 2010 article in *The Guardian,* retailers are producing clothing styles "that target children and encourage premature sexualization" of young girls (theguardian.com/society/2010/apr/16/children-clothing-survey-bikini-heels [02-03-15]).

If possible, begin your conversations about dressing modestly before fashion becomes a priority for your daughter. Some preschool-aged girls are already concerned with every piece of clothing they put on, while others are still throwing on whatever is most comfortable well into their teen years. Help yours embrace her individual taste. While it's important that your daughter be comfortable in her clothes and confident in her appearance, she doesn't need every one of the latest styles, even if "everyone else is wearing it" and especially if the clothes project an image that's a mismatch to her true identity and inner beauty.

Courtney began finding books in the girls' and youth sections of the Christian bookstore that specifically addressed the beauty of dressing modestly and the importance of self-respect for her body as a temple of the Holy Spirit. **"Do you not know that your body is a temple of the Holy Spirit within you, whom you have from God? You are not your own, for you were bought with a price. So glorify God in your body"** (1 Corinthians 6:19–20). She learned that girls often dress provocatively just to seek attention in a misguided attempt to feel good about themselves and attractive to others. Unfortunately, the attention they seek is often not the kind of attention they get. While nothing excuses a boy's rude remarks or inappropriate actions, girls of all ages need to be aware that guys are wired differently. While a girl may think, *That will make me look pretty*, a boy may see only sex appeal in her choice of clothing. Courtney says, "We need to keep Christ as the focus of our modesty. How dare we make our brothers stumble when what we wear could cause them to sin? In regard to my clothing choices, I have to consider not just how it could negatively affect me, but even more important, how it could affect others."

When your pretty princess is trying on clothes and making choices of her own, be sensitive about how you respond; don't be quick to react negatively. Help her see for herself what constitutes a good choice in modest dress. Choose your battles carefully, but know that there is a time to draw the line. Again, be the mom. You're the benevolent and nurturing queen of the palace, and she is your precious princess, still learning and growing. With God's help, you can establish rules and stick with them, even as you continue to model them. Explain why you have rules: for her good and her protection, as well as her witness.

A friend of mine was swimsuit shopping with her teenage girl. After her daughter had tried on a trendy new bikini, my friend said, "I'm sorry, honey, but I won't buy that suit for you."

"But Mom . . . " came a protest.

She explained herself, "I want your curves to be covered, top and bottom."

"But Mom . . . "

She could have chosen to please her daughter, giving in to her request. She chose instead the unpopular position of the moment, trusting it would reap rewards for the future. My friend went on to remind her daughter, as she had done in previous discussions, of the reasons why a more modest choice would be better. After further dialogue, my friend realized her daughter had chosen that swimsuit primarily for its color, not giving much thought to its coverage, its style, or the potential unwanted attention she could receive while wearing it. This still-maturing girl needed her mom's gentle-but-firm guidance to make a decision that was in her best interest.

SELF-IMAGE

For many women, self-image—the perception they have of themselves—is directly connected to their body weight. Whether we perceive ourselves as underweight or overweight, many of us are distracted by it, and if we allow our self-perception to be determined by our weight, we are falling into yet another trap!

I admit that I've been ensnared by this trap many times. Since I've struggled to be content with my weight and body image, I have risked allowing my own insecurity to be cast upon my daughter. If she perceives that I am confident only when my weight is ideal and that I am insecure when it's not, she has received a message of conditional acceptance of self. Seemingly harmless complaints about my size and shape have the potential to distort her views of her own body. According to Dr. Leslie Sim, a child psychologist and the clinical director of the eating disorders program at Mayo Clinic, "Moms are probably the most important influence on a daughter's body image." (www.usatoday.com/story/news/nation/moms-daughters-influence-body-image [01-31-15]).

Be careful with your choice of words. "Does this skirt make me look too skinny?" "I feel so frumpy!" "I just have to lose weight so I can look good again." What do little listening ears overhear from you concerning your image of yourself? Too often, society, peers, and even parents place too much emphasis on a growing girl's size and body shape, and this can have damaging effects and even long-term repercussions on her self-image. Seek God's guidance, and engage in healthy conversation with your daughter about body image. Ask her how she sees herself when she's making an appearance in front of the mirror. Affirm and encourage her in every aspect of her appearance, giving the glory to God for creating her just as He has.

APPEARING BEFORE THE MIRROR

What does your godly girl see when she looks into the mirror? You are by her side as she faces the awkward years of change; you're there to help her embrace the beauty God has given her, inside and out. Remind her that she is growing just as she is supposed to, even when her new front teeth are temporarily oversized for the rest of her face or when she feels that other body parts are growing too slowly or quickly for her comfort. Let her know you're there to listen. You may be her only trusted source of wisdom and advice concerning the most sensitive appearance issues as curves begin to form and acne appears out of nowhere.

From early on, you can develop dialogue and build a relationship specifically concerning sensitive image issues. Become the trusted go-to source of care, attention, and help as she begins noticing her physical appearance and the changes that she'll be more prepared to face and embrace with your loving attention, preparation, support, and unconditional acceptance, especially during the awkward preteen years. Continue to remind her that she is fearfully and wonderfully made in the image of God. She is changing and growing into the beautiful young woman that He designed her to become.

DON'T CONFORM—BE TRANSFORMED!

The world gives us unfair expectations and false definitions of beauty, conditioning us toward envy and vanity. It would have us believe that if we chase after one more thing in a quest for what it falsely defines as beauty, we will finally be content and happy with our appearance. If we're able to grasp that *one more thing*, we will find that there's *always* one more thing. Your daughter's needs cannot be determined by what she sees in the mall or hears in advertising. In our commerce-driven society, advertising's job is to tell her that her present appearance and her current possessions aren't good enough, so she needs more. Help your princess to disconnect herself from that which is distracting her to the point of discontent. Teach her to look with discerning eyes at the world's message concerning beauty and contentment and at the contrasting truth of God's Word, which tells her, **"Do not be conformed to this world, but be transformed by the renewal of your mind, that by testing you may discern what is the will of God, what is good and acceptable and perfect"** (Romans 12:2).

You are her example. Show your precious princess that she cannot find true happiness or contentment in her appearance, her possessions, or even her accomplishments. True contentment comes when we recognize the Holy Spirit's transforming work: **"I have learned in whatever situation I am to be content"** (Philippians 4:11). Be thankful for what you look like, for who you are in Christ, and for what you have (and don't have), grateful that He knows and provides what's best. Model this for her. And remind her that His Majesty provides all she needs: **"And my God will supply every need of yours according to His riches in glory in Christ Jesus"** (Philippians 4:19).

A WORD OF GRACE

In our image-driven world, we easily succumb to the pressure to make an appearance. How do we appear to our friends and our family? on social media? in front of the mirror? Because of our vain human nature, it's quite natural for us and for our daughters to desire the approval, admiration, and accolades of our peers concerning our appearance. We let it determine how we see ourselves, forgetting the one thing that matters most: our appearance before the Lord. We also fall into comparison traps, measuring ourselves against others and receiving only disappointment or disillusionment as a result.

For all the issues we have regarding appearance, topped with a faulty definition of vain beauty that the world has attempted to give us, oh, how we need a word of grace. And we have it! We receive by faith God's perfect Word, which tells us that our sins are forgiven by Christ's blood shed on the cross. Read again God's grace-filled words through the prophet Isaiah: **"Though your sins are like scarlet, they shall be as white as snow"** (Isaiah 1:18). We appear before the Lord cleansed, forgiven, and free in our Savior, Jesus Christ.

SHOW AND TELL

1. When your daughter catches you making an appearance before the mirror, what does she see in your expression and body language? Are you humbly pleased with your appearance, from the top of your head to the tips of your toes? Or does your expression reveal discontent or dislike? Pray for the ability to see yourself as God sees you, made beautiful in Christ. With His help, openly express a healthy self-image to your daughter, leading her by your example. Read about the Proverbs 31 woman, especially the last verse: **"Charm is deceitful, and beauty is vain, but a woman who fears the Lord is to be praised"** (Proverbs 31:30). And discuss.

2. Where do you see the greatest obstacles to your daughter's contentment regarding her physical appearance and her self-image? Are they found in competitive friends, comparison traps, social media, or other areas? Consider the truths you can share with her regarding true beauty, based on this chapter and the Scripture passages contained within it. Make a plan, relevant to her age and stage of growth, to both gently address the issues and encourage her in every area.

3. Plan a special mother-daughter shopping trip, during which you take the opportunity to examine fashions together, from the little girls' section of the store to the juniors' and women's departments. Talk about what it means to honor God with our bodies in reference to modest dress. Enjoy a dialogue date over lunch or a special treat to continue your discussion and affirm to her that she is growing beautifully as God's girl.

4. Talk with your growing girl about the kind of appearance she would like to make before others. Encourage her to be less concerned with her physical appearance or with impressing others and more concerned with her character and the opportunity she possesses to represent His Majesty, her heavenly Father, the one who defines her as "white as snow" and His precious child. Together, ask: "How and where can I reflect Your image today, Jesus?"

Chapter 8

Growing Pains—
Purpose for a Princess's Royal Pains

And we know that for those who love God all things work
together for good, for those who are called according to His
purpose. Romans 8:28

STRETCHED FOR A PURPOSE

*M*y sweet princess tiptoed into our royal
bedroom in the middle of the night, softly whimper-
ing. Coming to me, she cried, "Mom, help! My legs
ache so much I can't sleep!" In a half-asleep stupor
that night, like so many others, I rubbed her legs,
which were literally stretching out beneath her! Once
I was more awake, I reminded her that her leg aches
were actually growing pains, an uncomfortable albeit
necessary part of physical growth. Her aching legs
were a telltale sign of a quickly growing body.

The early chapters of Courtney's life story, like that of every
growing girl, contain other types of growing pains too.

Pain that all too often accompanies emotional and spiritual growth, pain in relationships and circumstances that may be uncomfortable or even unbearable. But necessary? Does life have to hurt? We would like to think not; however, sometimes the greatest growth happens through painful experiences. And whether or not they realize it, our daughters are being *stretched* for a purpose.

As your daughter grows in all ways, physically, emotionally, and spiritually, so you, too, are given the chance to grow (and you will!). In fact, you'll be *stretched* regularly, and with your growth will come your own pains. During my twin pregnancy, my abdomen grew so quickly that I experienced the kind of growing pain that left permanent signs behind. My skin was stretched in such a way that it left telltale marks as a reminder of the lives that grew within me. Maybe you can relate. Stretch marks, like memories, may remain as reminders that the stretching served a purpose. So when you're facing difficulties in the day-to-day demands of parenting or you're hurting for her as you see her struggle, remember that there is a purpose for your pain, whether or not you have a tangible reminder of it. You are not being stretched in vain or for no reason. Like your princess, you are a work in progress in the sometimes painful process of being molded and transformed into His image.

Your princess's life story will inevitably include growing pains across every chapter. Although her life may not contain the plotline of the best-known and beloved tales, it will contain action and adventure and a good share of drama and conflict, like it or not. As your daughter grows, she will learn that there is an element of mystery to her life story too, since she won't always be able to see the purpose to what she is going through. But you can remind her that there is a point to every paragraph and that the author of her life and faith has a plan that is continually unfolding as the pages are turned.

His Majesty doesn't want your daughter to have difficulty. But in this not-so-fairy-tale, fallen, and sinful world, she WILL have trouble because she struggles with sin like everyone else. Jesus said, **"In the world you will have tribulation. But take heart; I have overcome the world"** (John 16:33). Get that? We will have tribulation. It is part of life under the cross. But she has Jesus' promise that He has triumphed over every tribulation and trouble, so even when she wishes she could simply hit the delete key, you can remind her that every detail can and will be used as part of a much deeper, broader story that may or may not be fully realized in her lifetime.

None of us can delete or erase those sections smeared by sin. We recognize that, while some of our problems come as consequences of our sin, other problems come through no fault of our own but as part of living in a sin-ridden, messed-up world. No matter the cause, we have the promise of God's forgiveness in Christ; we have His help and His restoration. He can take the most messed-up storyline and redeem it, for He has overcome the world by His death and resurrection. We are redeemed! And by faith, we are overcomers too! **"Everyone who believes that Jesus is the Christ has been born of God . . . everyone who has been born of God overcomes the world. And this is the victory that has overcome the world— our faith"** (1 John 5:1, 4).

How do you help your daughter walk through the difficult chapters, when her plotline is thicker and more complex than you'd ever thought possible and you wonder how to help her get through it? A friend of mine shared her daughter's most difficult chapter to date:

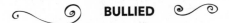 BULLIED

Anna was a friendly fifth-grade student who loved learning, enjoyed her classmates, and was eager to participate in her first year of sports at school. Unfortunately, she sustained an unrelated injury early in the year, which took her out of sports for the season and began an unexpected chain of events that led the other girls in Anna's class to start ignoring her and leaving her out. This was devastating to Anna, who'd never had friend issues until then. *One* girl in particular singled her out and began bullying her. Whenever Anna tried to talk to other classmates, the bully would lead them away, intentionally leaving Anna by herself. She was left to sit alone at the lunch table, and she endured mean looks and snotty exchanges in the halls and bathrooms throughout the day.

Eventually, Anna was sobbing herself to sleep every single night, wondering what she had done and what was wrong with her that she didn't have friends anymore. Her mother remembers, "I spent hours listening to her and trying to help her come up with solutions and new things to try. We tried to have playdates and sleepovers. Nothing was working. I finally told Anna she HAD to speak to the teacher about it." Anna meekly shared the situation with her teacher, who was very receptive and kept a watchful eye.

As time went on, the sports season came to a close. At the awards party, Anna received the Most Dedicated Player award for showing up to all practices and games and cheering her teammates on, though her injury prevented her from playing. Anna's mom recalls, "I saw how excited she was; I witnessed the tears of joy run down her face—joy that was immediately taken away by the meanest, nastiest look from the bully when Anna returned to her seat. She cried more than ever when she went to sleep that night, and I decided that I needed to step in."

Anna's mom, also a teacher in the school, talked with the principal and Anna's teacher. She contacted the mother of the bully, hoping they could work through the situation together. The teacher talked with girls in the class and found out they were scared of the bully and too afraid to befriend Anna for fear of retaliation. The bully's parents waged an all-out war on the school and especially on Anna and her mother. The bully's family was very outspoken and turned everything around, blaming Anna and attempting to make her look like she was the worst child ever; they claimed her mother was harassing their family, and they wanted her fired. "I have never felt as surrounded by pure evil as I did at that time. It was the most gut-wrenching time of my entire life. *I know that the devil was working overtime* against our school, my family, and me."

Although the bully's family eventually left the school, my friend struggled with unresolved feelings and resultant pain for a long time. "I know that my daughter was not the worst child ever; in fact, she taught me how to live my faith in the eye of the storm. She and

I prayed many prayers together. We talked about our faith and how God can work through even the toughest of times. We cried together. We studied the Bible together." Anna cut out Bible passages from church bulletins and taped them to her mirror, and she clung to the words of the contemporary Christian song "Overcomer," listening to it over and over and receiving hope that she would overcome this, by faith, just as Jesus promised, during a time when there didn't seem to be any hope. Looking back, Anna's mother rejoiced, "God brought her through!"

When the next school year began, Anna found that she had all her old friends back. Maybe they, too, grew through the painful circumstances of the previous year. God redeemed Anna's messed-up storyline. The One who overcame the world enabled her to overcome too. He provided help and restoration, and He used Anna's mother in powerful ways to hold up, help, and guide His precious princess throughout the ordeal.

By God's gentle grace, Anna was able to live her faith, and it got her through a very difficult time. She and her family try not to focus on why God allowed this or other painful circumstances to happen to them, but they consider, instead, how God can use their trials for good, how He protects them, and how He will always be with them through all things.

WHY ME?

Maybe your daughter's growing pains include struggles with friends, or maybe they're academic. Perhaps she's been sick a lot or she's been treated unfairly by a teacher or other authority figure. She may have been ridiculed for her faith or suffered a loss. She may be adjusting to a major move or a change in family dynamics. Maybe she is crying out, "Why me, God? I didn't ask for this. Why have You allowed this?" And perhaps all she sees is the apparent impossibility of her situation, the unfairness of it, or the pain or frustration in it. Be gentle as she endures such growing pains. Recognize that they are real. Listen more than you speak. Ask God for timing and discernment as you offer the very real comfort of your presence and, even better, the reassuring truth from His Word—not offered tritely with a nonchalant "this too shall pass," but with sincerity that reveals your own trust in God, in spite of and in the midst of difficult circumstances and the most tender growing pains. Seek His direction if you're called to take action on behalf of or alongside your daughter.

Maybe right now, as your precious princess stares into the face of her own circumstances or those of someone close to her, she struggles to see anything clearly. But one day, the Lord promises, she will see clearly and understand fully. **"For now we see in a mirror dimly, but then face to face. Now I know in part; then I shall know fully, even as I have been fully known"** (1 Corinthians 13:12). As you share these words with her, explain that when this verse was written, a mirror was a piece of polished brass, as evidenced by many archaeological finds. It was not able to provide a clear or perfect image like the mirrors we peer into today. What an appropriate illustration of our limited understanding and knowledge in each and every situation we face. Perhaps someday, your daughter will understand better than she does now; but one day—in heaven—when she peers into Jesus' face, she will know fully, even as He knows her fully now.

To see meaning and purpose beyond this page and in this moment is to look with eyes of faith. Help your daughter understand that she doesn't have to deny the tough present realities to trust that there is more to life than what meets her eyes in the present paragraph. Encourage her to talk to Jesus and approach His Majesty's throne of grace with her. Seek His help, comfort, deliverance, and peace. The Lord tenderly tells both of you, **"Call upon Me in the day of trouble; I will deliver you, and you shall glorify Me"** (Psalm 50:15).

When she is crying out, "Why me, God?" ask the Savior to give her eyes to see beyond her circumstances and courage to say, "Why not me? He loves me enough to guide me through anything this messed-up world tries to throw at me. He loves me enough to allow these struggles so that I may see my need for my Savior and learn to rest in His strength (not my own), even as He may use these struggles to sharpen my character and give me growth in Him." In this world, she will have troubles, but the soothing balm of His grace is much greater than the worst growing pain. He overcame sin, death, and the devil at the cross for her, His chosen child. Meanwhile, you can also teach her the following:

 1. GIVE GOD THANKS AND PRAISE!
Teach your princess, by your words and your example, that she can live a life of thanksgiving and gratitude, even in the midst of her growing pains. **"Give thanks in all circumstances; for this is the will of God in Christ Jesus for you"**

(1 Thessalonians 5:18). He is always worthy of her thanks and praise, in every chapter and on every page of her life story.

In the midst of each growing pain, you can gently remind your daughter that she is richly blessed. Even when it would be easier for her to focus on the painful parts, help her to dwell on those things for which she can give thanks: **"Whatever is true, whatever is honorable, whatever is just, whatever is pure, whatever is lovely, whatever is commendable, if there is any excellence, if there is anything worthy of praise, think about these things"** (Philippians 4:8). She can look for the truth even when she's surrounded by lies. She can find at least one thing that is just when so much seems wrong. She can focus on something that is pure when life's situations are tainted. She can look for one lovely thing in the middle of her unlovely situation.

Guide her to see the blessings of God in every big and little thing:

- Tell her again how she is deeply loved by her family. (What an opportunity to recall fun family moments and special acts of kindness of which she's been the recipient.)

- Remind her of the encouraging words of a favorite teacher, the laughter of a faithful friend, the hugs of Grandma, or the love of a pet.

- Help her think of the delicious foods she loves to eat, the changing of the seasons and the fun activities each brings, and the continual provision by God of all her needs.

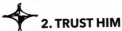 Above all, rejoice with her in God's gift of faith in Jesus, her Prince of Peace. He is her risen and living Lord and Savior! He has chosen and redeemed her, and He lives in her today!

In response to God's generous provision and endless blessings, together you can thank and praise Him! **"Blessed be the God and Father of our Lord Jesus Christ, who has blessed us in Christ with every spiritual blessing in the heavenly places"** (Ephesians 1:3).

2. TRUST HIM

Let her know that God will work through this and every detail of her life for her spiritual good and for His purpose. **"And we know that for those who love God all things work together for good, for those who are called according to His purpose"** (Romans 8:28). Even when she may not understand what that purpose is, she can know that He is completely capable and absolutely faithful and will carry her through the most difficult situations. By the Spirit's power, she can acknowledge Him as her Lord and Savior, trusting Him in the midst of the very things she cannot make sense of. **"Trust in the Lord with all your heart, and do not lean on your own understanding. In all your ways acknowledge Him, and He will make straight your paths"** (Proverbs 3:5–6).

Someone once told me to look for the blessing in the mess. Guide your girl to look for the blessing in a difficult, stressful, or frustrating situation—not because she's making light of it, but because she's shifting her outlook, with God's help. Maybe together you can refer to her growing pains as "growth opportunities" as she learns to trust God in the midst of her trials. She may even start looking for ways in which God is working these tough times for eventual good:

🌼 Maybe she messes up during a recital or performance, and another child, blessed to see that he's not alone in his mishaps, is encouraged to try again.

🌼 Maybe she was blamed for something she didn't do and learns the humbling lesson that life isn't fair as she responds graciously. In addition, others are blessed as they witness her humble example and learn from it.

🌼 Maybe she was ridiculed repeatedly by a former friend, and she's now blessed with growth in character and greater empathy for others, recognizing how much words can hurt.

🌼 And on a lighter note, maybe she burns the entire batch of cookies in her first attempt to bake alone and is blessed later to see her hungry siblings graciously eating them anyway.

✦ 3. KEEP AN ETERNAL PERSPECTIVE

In this and every chapter of her life story, your beloved daughter will suffer a great number of growing pains. She will not find perfect justice, fairness, or goodness in this sin-stained world. But in the day of Christ Jesus, when He returns to deliver His child to her eternal home in His kingdom, every growing pain, every trial and trouble, will cease to exist! Share with your princess the eternal perspective of the apostle Paul, who suffered great pain, injustice, and hardship as He worked to spread the Gospel. Paul was led by the Holy Spirit to proclaim: **"For I consider that the sufferings of this**

present time are not worth comparing with the glory that is to be revealed to us" (Romans 8:18). Nothing can compare to the glory of the Lord, which will be revealed in us when we are gathered around His heavenly throne!

CONSIDER THE CONTEXT

As your daughter stretches into the teen years, there may be times when it seems no matter what you say or do, you'll receive an eye roll, an impatient sigh, a "Mom, you're so clueless" response. While a disrespectful retort is inappropriate and should be gently reprimanded, consider the context. Is she struggling between the past, when she saw herself as Mommy's little imitator, and the future, when she hopes to see herself as a mature young adult who is independent and able to think for herself? The period of psychological, emotional, and spiritual growth between the two is huge. Think back to your own teen years, and recall the confusion and uncertainty of that period. Be sensitive to her rash responses, recognizing these as a type of growing pain as well and remembering the old adage that "this, too, shall pass."

THE PAIN OF CONSEQUENCES

Led by God's Word, you are teaching your impressionable princess right from wrong; you're establishing rules and creating clear-cut boundaries, all for her good and in her best interest, that she may live a **"self-controlled, upright, and godly"** life in Christ (Titus 2:12). And when she walks out the palace door, others in authority are doing likewise. What may happen when she chooses wrong instead of right, breaks the rules, or defiantly steps outside the boundaries?

Sometimes, the growing pains she endures are the direct or indirect consequences of poor choices and mistakes she has made. What can you teach her? Just as in other difficulties, let her know that God is worthy of her continual thanks and praise in the midst of these circumstances too, and she can trust that He will use *even these* for good and for growth. She can cling to His promise of grace and forgiveness that are hers in Christ.

So often, we'd like to step in and save the day, sparing our daughters the pain associated with consequences, but we need to ask ourselves if intervening is the best thing we can do for our growing girls when they've strayed from the path. A wise mentor and friend shared her years of experience with me, saying, "When you've guided your girl on the right path and yet she makes a poor decision, don't excuse it away; let her experience the consequence of that decision. While you may be tempted to say, 'I told you so,' don't. The fact that she is coming to you as she faces her consequences means she already knows. With God's help, you've taught her well. So instead say, 'Tell me about it.' And keep her words strictly confidential." Help her learn through her mistakes, and with your guidance, she'll recognize right from wrong more fully through the natural or imposed consequences of her choice. By God's grace, she will even grow as a result!

THE POEM

Courtney's primary school was preparing to publish a poetry book during her second grade year. She was a good little writer, but struggled to think creatively on the very day she was told she had to come up with something for possible submission for the book; suddenly, a poem came to mind that her cousin had recited to her, insisting it was his own creation. Courtney rationalized that no one would ever know, since it was written by a relative who lived four states away. She jotted it down and handed it to her teacher, who was amazed by the poem and insisted that it go into the book.

A few days later, Courtney was leafing through a borrowed Shel Silverstein book of poetry, and she found the very piece that her cousin had claimed as his own. She began to panic! That night, she came to my room, unable to sleep. "Mom, my stomach hurts," she whimpered.

"Does it feel like a knot?" I asked. She nodded vehemently. "Are you nervous about something?" I continued. (I'd hit the mark without even realizing it.)

"No!" she insisted nervously. After attempting to comfort her with a few more words, I sent her back to bed.

As she began to doze off, the words of an original poem started to take shape in her head. The next day, she put them to paper and turned in the creation, saying to her teacher, "I want to replace the other poem with this one."

As Courtney recalls this memory, she considers it a major learning experience. She shouldn't have stolen another person's work, whether it was her cousin's or a published author's. Although she was able to correct her wrongdoing on her own and didn't receive external consequences, she faced her own inner battle, a consequence in its own right. She said, "It tore me apart inside. I was distraught. The whole in-cident showed me the extent of how badly I feel when I know I've done something wrong. It was character-forming. And I've never plagiarized anything since." She knew the Lord was working in her young life as the Holy Spirit convicted her of her sin and she confessed it to her Savior. She had learned right from wrong by God's Word, and this painful incident provided a growth opportunity to live out what she had learned.

IT'S OKAY TO SEEK HELP

Sometimes, our daughters' difficulties can't be easily fixed. At these times, you may be at wit's end, wondering how to help your daughter through a particularly painful time. Please consider that you may not always be able to give your daughter all the help she needs. Prayerfully contemplate if or when you need to seek professional help. You are not a failure as a parent when you seek help beyond what you're able to give at home; in fact, you're acting in her best interest. The Lord provides His people with godly professionals whose gifts and training enable them to assist families in tangible, impactful ways. Look for signs of ongoing anxiety or depression, such as a withdrawal from activities or interests or prolonged changes in eating or sleeping habits. Seek God's strength to face difficult situations, acknowledging them instead of ignoring or glossing over them, since many issues grow worse without intervention. Communicate openly with your husband about your concerns; together, search for a trusted Christian counselor, seek the guidance of your pastor, or both.

Through every trial and tribulation, the Lord walks with you, your precious princess, and the entire royal family. And you have His promise that, in every struggle, He is growing you through the pain. Just look at what He is producing: **"We rejoice in our sufferings, knowing that suffering produces endurance, and endurance produces character, and character produces hope, and hope does not put us to shame, because**

God's love has been poured into our hearts through the Holy Spirit who has been given to us" (Romans 5:3–5).

What's in store in the following pages of your princess's life story? We are unable to read ahead; only the Lord knows what's to follow. With the certainty of eternal life, where she and all her loved ones in Christ will be gathered around the heavenly Father's throne of grace, He gives her the strength and the joy to live this chapter—even when it's filled with growing pains—to the fullest!

DON'T CONFORM–BE TRANSFORMED!

Continually point your princess to God's Word of truth, even when giving up or going the way of the world would seem to her to be the easier option, especially when the ache of growing pains is severe and the world is whispering subtle lies: "Do you really have to listen to the Bible's words anymore, especially in THIS difficult circumstance?" "What is truth, anyway? It may be different for everyone." (Don't be surprised if she hears lies like these even at an early age.) Drown out every lie as you share with her that God's Word IS truth—the only absolute truth. We would be wise to listen to His every word, each of which is completely relevant to us today, just as it was when God inspired each writer to pen each page. His inerrant Holy Word is the perfect and final authority for our lives in every circumstance. Warn her that, because she may not always like what God has to say, it may be very tempting to dismiss some of Scripture because it is not in line with the world's way of thinking, what today's culture tries to dictate, or what her circumstance has driven her or others to do. And then remind her of His forgiveness for the times she listened to the lies of the culture or conformed to the patterns of this world; thank the Holy Spirit for His work, enabling you and her to cling to God's absolute truth and to be transformed by it, able to discern His perfect will. **"Do not be conformed to this world, but be transformed by the renewal of your mind, that by testing you may discern what is the will of God, what is good and acceptable and perfect"** (Romans 12:2).

A WORD OF GRACE

When growing pains hit, do we cry out, "Why me?" and then allow ourselves to remain stuck there, focused only on ourselves and our pain? Maybe we've inadvertently taught our daughters to do that. Maybe we stare at our stretch marks, our memories and reminders of difficult times, and see only the pain that caused them, forgetting to look for growth through them or the beauty that may be found in them. We fail to trust that God can work through our growing pains to bless us and others. We neglect to see the bigger picture or other people's pain because we're completely absorbed by *our* situation and *our* pain.

God knows our hurt. He knows the sins we struggle with that are connected to each and every growing pain, and He knows we cannot get ourselves unstuck. As in every other area of life, we desperately need God's grace, and we receive it at the cross of Christ. **"In Him we have redemption through His blood, the forgiveness of our trespasses [sins], according to the riches of His grace, which He lavished upon us"** (Ephesians 1:7–8). His forgiveness frees us to take our focus off ourselves and look to Him for peace in the middle of our pain. In His strength, we can see our stretch marks as the result of times of growth, trusting God to work through them, even if we may never see or fully understand His purpose. By His grace, **"which He lavished upon us,"** we're able to see the bigger picture and share it with our precious daughters.

SHOW AND TELL

1. Our Savior delivers us from our troubles. He is our source of wisdom and knowledge. He strengthens us and comforts us, and His Spirit guides us into all truth. He promises all this, and so much more, in His Word. Share the following verses with your growing girl during troubled times (or *any* time) and help her find the promises I've just shared, as recorded here: Proverbs 2:6; Psalm 34:17; Philippians 4:13, 2 Corinthians 1:3–4; and John 16:13.

2. Make or purchase a batch of play clay or something similar. Take your daughter to God's Word in Isaiah 64:8: **"But now, O Lord, You are our Father; we are the clay, and You are our potter; we are all the work of Your hand."** As you work the clay together, remind her that she is a work in progress, like clay in the Master Potter's hands. And while the bending, stretching, and reshaping may be uncomfortable, He is molding her into the shape He has in mind for her, to accomplish His purpose for her life, for good and to His glory!

3. Create a unique version of a growth chart for your daughter. Instead of recording physical growth in height, let this chart be a go-to place to record emotional, intellectual, and spiritual growth. You may want to include milestone events that celebrate growth (confirmation, graduation, etc.), but be mindful of the large growth spurts that happened as a result of a period of pain.

They're not as obvious to track, but so significant to recall and remember for continued growth and for the opportunity to stop and say thanks to God in each and every circumstance.

4. In chapter 5, *Before the Throne,* I encouraged you to begin a prayer journal and to give one to your daughter too. Write out your prayers, and lift them to the Lord during your daughter's difficult times and in the midst of her growing pains. Because they're recorded, you're much more likely to look back and recognize answers that you, your daughter, or others have received. God can use this discipline to increase your trust while reminding you that His current care is just as reliable as His care in the past. *Review* answered prayers with your princess and the entire royal family. *Remind* them of God's grace throughout every situation. And *rejoice* together in the salvation that's yours in Christ!

Chapter 9

Your Presence Is Requested—
Being There for Your
Princess

She looks well to the ways of her household . . . her children rise
up and call her blessed. Proverbs 31:27–28

THE HONOR OF YOUR PRESENCE

"*The* he princess *requests the honor of the*
queen's presence." Could this be a royal announce-
ment from a treasured fairy tale, or could it be the
request of a real-life princess who resides with you
in your humble palace? You're a central character
in her life story, and your physical presence enables
you to provide for her needs, with God's help. Even
more important, by His grace, you're able to *be there*
for her, providing her with your loving presence by
your words and your touch, by your invested time and
interest, and by your guiding hand, which holds hers.

HOLDING HANDS

Think, for a moment, what it means to hold hands with your daughter as you walk across page after page of your life stories together. Your comforting touch soothes her fears and provides her with the reassurance of your physical presence while also providing protection and guidance. You lead and she follows, with her hand safely in the grip of yours. Now consider for a moment that your heavenly Father also holds your hand. He leads and you follow; His touch comforts your fears, protects you at all times, and guides you through every chapter of your story. Even when you lose your grip, you are firmly in His! In Isaiah 41:13, God says, **"For I, the Lord your God, hold your right hand; it is I who say to you, 'Fear not, I am the one who helps you.'"** The psalmist declares to the Lord, **"Nevertheless, I am continually with You; You hold my right hand"** (Psalm 73:23).

As your heavenly Father continually holds you by your right hand, and as you have the awesome privilege and responsibility of holding your daughter's hand, He holds hers too. Your very presence—your loving and comforting touch upon her life—will be felt long after you've stopped physically holding her hand. You can't always have her by the hand, but rest in the fact that He does; her name is even engraved on the palms of His hands (Isaiah 49:16).

THE TOUCH OF LOVE

What momma doesn't love to hug, hold hands, and cuddle with her little ones? As a young mom, I learned the importance of positive physical touch during a parents' Bible class, so my husband and I intentionally nurtured our children with large doses of positive physical touch. Back scratches quickly became the favorite for our royal family. I scratched backs while snuggled in the rocking chair during story time or family devotions; while sitting on the side of their beds, listening to their prayers and tucking them in; and while seated side by side on the sofa, during family movie nights.

It was a special touch of love.

The comforting back scratch routine that began at home grew into a pattern during worship in church. With a child on each side and the third one still within reach, I spent countless hours in the pew gently patting and scratching backs, which calmed these active youngsters and helped them learn to focus and listen.

Your daughter will benefit from your gentle touch of love, and God will use it powerfully! As a little girl, she may want to be held when she is tired, scared, or hurt. As a growing girl, she can relax in your calming, warm embrace after a stressful day of school. Your teenage girl will respond to the blessing of your gentle squeeze on her shoulder as you say, "I'm here for you." At any age, she may reach for a hug when she's excited and when she's sad because your touch of love is something special.

As you provide healthy doses of positive physical touch, tell her of Jesus' touch. His touch of love was felt by the world. Our Savior's hand reached out again and again to calm, to bless, and to heal. When Peter and John fell facedown, terrified, during Christ's transfiguration, He came to His disciples, touched them, and calmed them, saying, **"Have no fear"** (Matthew 17:7). People brought little children to Jesus that He might touch them. (They knew His touch was something special!) **"And He took [the children] in His arms and bless-ed them, laying His hands on them"** (Mark 10:16). As Jesus placed His powerful hands upon the sick and the diseased, the lame and the blind, they were miraculously healed. Tell your precious princess again how Jesus reached out and touched the world with His sacrificial love as He died and rose to take away their sins. Jesus' ultimate touch of redeem-ing love enables you to reach out and touch your precious daughter with His love too. His hand reaches out and holds your hand and hers today. (See again Psalm 73:23.)

TEACHABLE MOMENTS

Your days are full of teachable moments about life, faith, and values. Remember the Lord's commands in Deuteronomy 6? **"Talk of them when you sit in your house."** I encouraged you in chapter 3 to make time for the precious priority of learning from God's Word through personal and family devotions. In addition, your time spent together around the table, at work and at play, and in everyday life can be faith- and character-building times as you recognize countless teachable moments and opportunities to impart God's wisdom to her, applying it to each conversation and situation, if possible. **"Come, O children, listen to me; I will teach you the fear of the LORD"** (Psalm 34:11). Be on the alert for unexpected moments and spontaneous discussion starters in the midst of everyday life; seize these opportunities.

MEALTIME

When you **"sit in your house,"** you may quite literally sit around the table. If you are not in the practice of having mealtime together, I encourage you to make the time. Even if crazy schedules mean you have to shift mealtime or it can't happen every single day, plan for it as often as possible. Whether your princess sits in the royal high chair or is nearly grown and ready to leave the palace, she will benefit from this nurturing time together. She and her siblings have the gift of the queen's and king's presence—your full attention.

★ Mealtime is a perfect opportunity to pray together as a family. As she is able, let your growing girl and each family member take turns leading prayers. Our family often prayed a common table prayer, but we also modeled and encouraged spontaneous prayers, specific to that day's provision and protection, with praise and thanksgiving for the meal and the day, whatever it contained.

★ Mealtime creates an environment of rest from the day, where the satisfaction of food and the security of faith and family can provide an atmosphere that encourages open communication. As our kids grew, we urged them to talk about their day, and we began sharing what we called *School Stories* and *High Point/Low Point*. Before they left the table, they were to share something significant, including a good and a not-so-good moment from the day. More often than not, a topic would come up that prompted our family to talk about important matters like forgiveness, helping others, the significance of our beliefs and values, and so much more.

★ Mealtime can be your time to show her the priority of her presence with you. Establish some protective boundaries for mealtime. All cell phones can be silenced and set away from the table, the TV and other media can be turned off, and other distractions can be kept to a minimum for everyone's benefit.

PLAYTIME

Don't wait for so-called *spare time*; instead, *make time* for play, prioritizing it in your family's schedule when possible. Playtime together develops communication skills and nurtures relationships. And playtime involving activities and games also promotes teamwork, sportsmanship, perseverance, and patience. Playtime can even prompt your daughter toward a continued desire to spend time with her family as she gets older. So prayerfully consider making playtime a priority.

★ Look for activities and games that involve the entire family and take an hour or less. They might be played inside or outside, and you may or may not choose to keep score. Consider including games that also teach about values and faith in the midst of the fun. Some family board games even involve Bible-learning strategies while engaging several ages at once.

★ Develop a regularly-scheduled *Family Night*. Place it on the calendar, or choose an evening of the week that will work most consistently over time so everyone knows that it's coming and can anticipate its arrival. *Suggestions:* Play a game. Read aloud an action-packed book. Sing along and dance to music with a positive or Christian message. Pop popcorn and view a favorite family movie. Afterward, discuss what you learned, read, or viewed in light of God's grace and His will for our lives. Teach your growing girl how to look for and discern the meaning and messages behind the stories, lyrics, and plot lines.

★ Start your own family traditions. On holidays, birthdays, and plain-old regular days, you can establish your own memorable traditions and mini celebrations that your daughter will want to repeat year after year or time after time. *Suggestions:* Have an impromptu variety show during which even the dog or cat gets to perform its talents. Build a snow family in the yard. Bake cookies and share them with neighbors. Plant flowers. Visit a water park or a zoo. Go out for ice cream. Go camping. Take a trip to an apple orchard or pumpkin patch. Drive to look at Christmas lights. Go caroling in the neighborhood. Revel in the joy shared while spending time in one another's presence!

TASK TIME

Consider the most basic hands-on tasks and activities that you must accomplish in a given week. Sometimes those tasks seem endless, and they're almost instantly undone. When you wonder if you're accomplishing anything of lasting value, remember that every moment of your presence, even in the menial tasks and constant clean-ups, makes a difference for your daughter that far outlasts the freshly-cleaned laundry or the momentarily-made beds. And you can involve her in age-appropriate ways. You're modeling a work ethic, loving care, and a desire to bless others and place their needs ahead of your own. Consider the blessed woman described in Proverbs 31: **"She looks well to the ways of her household and does not eat the bread of idleness. Her children rise up and call her blessed"** (vv. 27–28). In the presence of your daughter, you can make the most of every task.

✶ Work together, side by side, teaching her as you do. Give her responsibilities, and hold her accountable as she learns how to clean, complete laundry, create meals, shop for groceries, run errands, and more.

★ Be creative! Design a simple chart and offer realistic goals and rewards where appropriate. Let her tackle projects that she may not initially complete to your usual specifications; be careful to offer encouragement and praise for her earnest attempts. Show her that you trust her as you allow her to keep trying, and give her space to add her own creative touch. (One day, when Courtney was nine years old, she responded to my request that she set the table by wrapping the silverware and cutting small paper flowers to adorn each of our plates. And I was serving leftovers!)

★ With your mother-touch, you can teach her other life skills. You're training your little protégée to be a *chemist* when you teach her to bake (a favorite memory in our palace), allowing her to measure, mix, and create unique concoctions. You're training her to be an *artist* as you make crafty projects together. You're raising a *nurse* when you teach her how to tend to boo-boos, and you're training a *teacher* when you impart all kinds of information to her.

Your presence combined with your instruction will not only fulfill the request she has for "the honor of your presence," but she will also learn invaluable life skills that will help *her* achieve eventual independence and will help *you* accomplish immediate tasks or fun projects at the same time.

ANY TIME

Delight in each day with your daughter! Consider how a young child lives in the moment, enjoying it for what it is, and emulate that attitude. Resist the urge to say, "Mommy-hood will be so much easier when [you fill in the blank] is over!" (You might fill it in with anything from potty training to driver's education, from packing the diaper bag for her to packing boxes with her as she leaves for college or a career.) When my children were very small, a dear mentor and friend of mine listened to my woes. "Will this parenting thing ever get easier? It just has to get easier!" I cried. The words came tumbling from my mouth following several sleepless nights, when I wondered if I would ever accomplish more than cleaning up messes, folding laundry, and feeding little mouths. My friend's tender response was "Oh, Deb, parenting doesn't get easier; the difficulty is just different." She had loved every minute of her children's youth, but recognized the realities and the difficulties that were a part of each age and stage.

Don't be tempted to wish away the days, even the difficult ones. It's in the difficult days that we often learn the most. And what about the current schedule, activities, and commitments with your daughter that you may take for granted? Stop to notice and cherish the little things. Today will never come again. She will never be this age again. She will continue to change, maturing physically, emotionally, and spiritually, sometimes seemingly in the blink of an eye. Enjoy the present, and savor every season of parenting!

Don't wait for the weekend or holiday to spend a little one-on-one time with your daughter. Even a brief while in the evenings is significant. *Suggestions:* Create fun moments together. Spread out a picnic blanket in the middle of the living room floor. Trade back rubs, or give each other manicures. Go on an outing. Read a mom-and-daughter devotion, and receive the blessing and guidance provided through that nugget of truth for both of you. Live each day as though it is the last opportunity you have to impact her world for Christ:

"This is the day that the Lord has made; let us rejoice and be glad in it" (Psalm 118:24).

BEING THERE

While we want to maximize the time we have with our daughters and squeeze in as much as possible, our presence is often appreciated the most during time spent simply being together. Your time speaks volumes to her, even when a word isn't spoken or when your mere presence allows her to open the door for communication when she's ready. Listen to every real-life adventure or drama that she is bursting to share. As you do, you are showing her preference and priority, choosing to spend your downtime with her to listen, to rest, to simply be together.

A close friend shared with me an especially important time when her presence had a profound impact upon her daughter and their relationship. "The first time my daughter had a huge struggle with a friend, she was very upset but would not talk about it. I sat next to her and just rubbed her back and played with her hair. After about an hour, she finally started talking. This was a huge breakthrough for our relationship. That night, we talked and talked. We sat on her bed and talked; we went to a drive-through in our PJs and sat in the parking lot and talked some more. I drove home, and we talked even longer in the driveway. It was a night I will never forget: the night she became comfortable talking to me about herself and the growing young woman she was becoming. I listened and listened, and that's what she needed. From that night on, our relationship only became stronger. She trusted me more as I continued to listen to her, not judge her, and not break confidentiality."

Your daughter needs to talk, and she needs to be heard. She needs to know that you care and understand, that you truly desire to be there for her when you can. You can make it clear that you're giving her your complete and undivided attention when you put down your phone, turn off the TV, stop what you are doing, and give her eye contact as you provide her with the opportunity to talk. Reflect back what you've heard, and offer open-ended questions when she's ready to receive them. "Tell me about . . . " "What do you think about that?" "How did it make you feel?" Pay attention to her nonverbal cues. Note the attitude and feelings behind her words. You'll often be able to detect the cues that reveal a great deal to you about what's really going on inside. Pray for the ability to give her an appropriate and helpful response. I have prayed frequently that God would guide my words, that they would help and not hurt my daughter or the situation. I pray for discernment about when to open my mouth and when I should keep it closed.

TALKING TO HER

My princess never seemed to tire of hearing my real-life childhood tales. Repeatedly, she would beg, "Tell me another story from when you were a kid, Mom!" I seized the opportunity when she was all ears to teach her about her heritage and to let her learn from the mistakes I had made. She was able to take away bits of wisdom from other people who had affected my life and my faith walk as I recollected their words and stories. As I openly shared the often humorous and sometimes poignant pieces of my past, she was able to envision me as a youngster too.

From the time your princess is young, you can initiate conversation. Make it a habit to talk honestly and transparently about all kinds of things. Be purposeful and pointed with all topics that come up. What tough topics need to be addressed regarding choices, friends, ethical principles, and moral absolutes? Prayerfully consider your timing, your opportunities, and the appropriate depth and purpose of your talk time. If open and honest communication becomes second nature when she's young, then it's more likely to continue well into the awkward preteen and teen years because the habit has been developed and, along with it, trust and comfort in your presence. That said, do not fret if you've not begun intentional conversations as soon as you would have liked. Begin where you are, trusting God to give you wisdom and guide your way as you talk and as you listen. Again, consider the traits of the blessed woman in Proverbs 31: **"She opens her mouth with wisdom, and the teaching of kindness is on her tongue"** (v. 26).

BETTER THAN A BEST FRIEND

Being there for your dear daughter does not mean being her best friend. She will have lots of friends who come in and go out of her life, but she will have only one mother whose God-given vocation is to nurture, discipline, and love as only a mother (not a buddy) can. In fact, it's unhealthy to seek to be her BFF, especially during her teen years when she needs your gentle but firm guidance, correction, and redirection. You can establish and build a close relationship, and you can still have fun together, laughing over inside jokes and sharing in shopping excursions, ice cream pit stops, and late-into-the-evening talks. In fact, you can make them even more special because you are her mom. You've known and nurtured her from infancy, and you love and accept her unconditionally;

you support and encourage her, and you continue to point her to Christ. You know things about her that her friends never will, and she trusts that you'll be there for her, even as friends may come and go. As she moves into adulthood, your relationship will likely appear more like that of two friends, but it's better because you'll always get to be her mom!

Your better-than-a-friend presence in her daily life makes all the difference as you tend to her basic needs and so much more. You are there for her when you sew the missing button on her best sweater, make her favorite meal, cheer for her from the bleachers or the sidelines, and help her with homework. *Your presence is requested*, that you may read every story that she writes, drive her to important activities, and clap with pride at her recitals and performances. (I can still picture Courtney performing on stage in the school musical, playing the keyboard during a recital, and entering the court during a middle-school basketball game. Although she kept her cool in front of her friends and other spectators, she sent repeated glances in our direction, quietly revealing her relief that her biggest advocates were there for her.)

YOUR PRESENCE

Your presence speaks louder than words when you're there for her greatest triumphs and her biggest crises. **"Rejoice with those who rejoice, weep with those who weep"** (Romans 12:15). I vividly recall a very difficult time for Courtney and for all of us. My husband had just accepted a call to serve as pastor of a church far away. His new position necessitated a cross-country move for our family in the middle of her sophomore year of high school. Although she had faced social struggles in her former high school, she also had very close

Christian friends and was actively involved in a vibrant youth group. Understandably, she was awfully upset about the move.

Courtney recalls being very angry and frustrated with her dad and me as we all settled into our new home. From her room, she thought, *I bet if I disappeared, they wouldn't even notice.* She huddled in the back of her closet and cried and cried. Later, she heard me holler for her when I hadn't seen her for a while. *Serves them right!* she thought. *But . . . I guess they do care enough to look for me.* I walked into her room, puzzled because I hadn't been able to find her anywhere, and then thought to search her closet. It broke my heart to see her tear-stained face when I found her hiding in the corner. Moved to tears, I talked for a bit, attempting to comfort her, and then I just sat on the floor of her bedroom as she continued to cry in the closet. My silent presence said more to her that day than my words could have. Although the weeks that followed were full of new faces and challenges, she knew the Lord was there for her and so were we.

GOD'S CONTINUAL PRESENCE–
ONCE UPON A TIME TO HAPPILY EVER AFTER

While you will not always be able to be physically present for your princess, your Savior never leaves her side. The psalmist says, **"Where shall I go from Your Spirit? Or where shall I flee from Your presence? If I ascend to heaven, You are there! If I make my bed in Sheol, You are there! If I take the wings of the morning and dwell in the uttermost parts of the sea, even there Your hand shall lead me, and Your right hand shall hold me"** (Psalm 139:7–10). From the moment He began knitting her together in the womb (Psalm 139:13), to her final breath in this life, to life forever with her Savior,

He is the Alpha and the Omega (Revelation 21:6), the first and the last, the beginning and the end. Our King reigns over all and is in all. He is all-powerful, all-knowing, and always-present. In and throughout His princess's life, He provides her with purpose and gives her courage, strength, and comfort for every page of her entire life story. Again in Psalm 139, the psalmist praises God, saying, **"in Your book were written, every one of them, the days that were formed for me, when as yet there was none of them"** (v. 16). You don't need to fear for your daughter in this life because her heavenly Father is with her through all of the days He formed for her. By the Holy Spirit's presence in her life, she'll receive all that she needs to live each day to the fullest, from once upon a time all the way to happily ever after with her Lord and Majesty in eternity.

DON'T CONFORM—BE TRANSFORMED!

The world attempts to conform us to itself, seeking to minimize the importance of a mother's presence in a daughter's life by focusing on the individual. How easily we can succumb to the lies of the world, the temptations of the devil, and our own sinful flesh, which may all lead us toward a place of self-interest so that even when we're physically present with our girls, our minds and our hearts are elsewhere, pursuing trivial matters and seeking petty diversions. If we become distracted and even consumed with our own needs, desires, and interests, we may fail to pay attention to what's going on in our daughters' lives. Once again, we look to God's wisdom in Romans 12:2: **"Do not be conformed to this world, but be transformed by the renewal of your mind, that by testing you may discern what is the will of God,**

what is good and acceptable and perfect." By His transforming power, we can live counterculturally, being fully present and attentive during our time together, placing our daughters' needs ahead of our own, and finding a healthy balance between our own and others' interests. By His Word, we can discern His good, acceptable, and perfect will in this (as in every) area of life: **"Do nothing from selfish ambition or conceit, but in humility count others more significant than yourselves. Let each of you look not only to his own interests, but also to the interests of others"** (Philippians 2:3–4).

A WORD OF GRACE

We are the queens and caretakers of our palace; we are the nurturers, the problem-solvers, the boo-boo fixers, the listeners, the advocates, the disciplinarians, the encouragers, the teachers . . . and more. We pour ourselves out for our growing girls, desiring to be personally present for them whenever possible, but so often, we fall short. Some days are harder than others. Accidents happen, feelings are hurt, disappointments occur, mistakes are made, deadlines loom, heavy demands are placed upon us at work and at home—everyone wants a piece of us. We feel completely drained. And it shows. We consider the overwhelming expectations for our presence, and some days we cry out, "I want to listen more carefully. I'd like to be more consistent with my encouragement. I desire to be more attentive to her needs. I want to help her fix what's broken. I would like to follow through with my discipline when she needs it. I need to forgive—again. But I am drained. Empty. I don't think I can give or do, share or fix, one more thing."

We may attempt to seek replenishment in any number of

worldly ways—physical rest, hobbies, exercise, time alone or with friends, and date night with our husband are all healthy ways to recharge. But when we are drained emotionally and spiritually, we can receive true and lasting replenishment only in our Lord. We need the lavish outpouring of God's grace upon us. We need to be refueled with His forgiveness, healing, and strength, and that comes to us through the Word and the Sacraments. The strength we have to raise our daughters, to give them our undivided attention, to be fully present when we're with them comes from the Lord. **"He gives power to the faint, and to him who has no might He increases strength . . . but they who wait for the Lord shall renew their strength"** (Isaiah 40:29–31).

As we soak up His Word and spend time in His continual presence, as we call upon Him in prayer, and as we come to His Table, we can trust that God will refill and refuel us, by the power of the Holy Spirit. God provides for us in every way we need, empowering and enabling us to pour ourselves out for the good of our daughters and others.

By His grace and strength, He is able to fill you with compassion when your daughter needs a listening ear, give you words of comfort and encouragement to share when she is hurting, and give you a generous heart to help in her times of need. The Lord infuses you with wisdom and knowledge that enable you to help where you can and fix what you can. He provides you with strength to follow through with discipline and with those demanding tasks and expectations that have been given to you. And He gives you the ability to forgive as He has first forgiven you. He **"is able to do far more abundantly than all that we ask or think, according to the power at work within us"** (Ephesians 3:20).

SHOW AND TELL

1. In this season of parenting, in what ways are you able to provide your momma touch for your growing girl? When do you see her reaching out for your touch, physically and in other ways? As you hold her hand and walk together across the early chapters of her life story, remind her continually of Jesus' ultimate touch—His redeeming love. She is safely in His grip.

2. Checking off items on our never-ending to-do lists may too easily become the measure of our days or evenings at home. Were they successful, productive, or efficiently spent? By what measure? Even when the items on our lists include our daughters, have we looked at an activity or task as something to get done so we could check our little box and get on with the next thing? When this happens to you, what can you do to shift your outlook, with God's help?

3. Teachable moments can be found as your princess receives the honor of your presence at meal time, play time, task time, or any time! Reflect upon these sections of this chapter, and consider one new way this week that you will set aside or create some together time.

4. How can you become more aware of the times when your daughter needs your complete and undivided attention? to simply be together? to talk and to hear a good word from you? Ask God to clear your eyes of distractions, opening them to her needs, that you may be fully present when you're present.

Chapter 10

Created by God's Design—
Purity for Her Prince

> Do you not know that your body is a temple of the Holy Spirit within you, whom you have from God? You are not your own, for you were bought with a price. So glorify God in your body.
> 1 Corinthians 6:19–20

GOD'S BEAUTIFUL CREATION

*T*ake a good look at the beautiful creation before you, your precious princess, created beautifully *female* by God's design and placed in your palace under your loving care. As you talk with her about God's Word of truth in the palace and beyond the palace gates, as you remind her of her unique identity in Christ, who has a special purpose and plan for her life, and as you create mother-daughter, queen-and-princess moments together, make it your priority to also communicate clearly God's plan for sexuality, as He so beautifully designed it to be set apart for marriage.

A TRUSTED RESOURCE–YOU

As you begin communicating this basic scriptural truth when she's young, you're laying down a solid foundation, and you build on it with related educational messages that you and others of godly influence share as she grows. The sad reality in our current culture is that she's likely to hear inappropriate and false information about sex long before you may consider her old enough for "the talk." Seek God's wisdom, draw from trusted resources, and gently begin dialogue at an early age. As you talk openly, you become a trusted resource when the difficult questions come. And they will come. Instead of asking, "Do you have questions?" ask, "What questions do you have?" You can be a safe place when she has questions about human development and sexuality. If you are the first person to teach her about this sensitive topic, she will weigh what others say against the foundational truth you've given her, and her moral compass will keep her on track as the Lord works in her life. As I taught my daughter these priceless truths, I learned that having "the talk" once-and-done isn't reality. Instead, ongoing dialogue and an open door of invitation to listen, speak, and respond are the norm.

Create opportunities to engage in conversation about her growing, maturing body, and look for teachable moments right in the middle of life. I enjoyed sharing with my daughter Christian resources that provided godly guidance for growing girls. I encourage you to find trusted resources, such as CPH's Learning about Sex series, with timely and applicable facts and engaging information for every age and stage of your daughter's development. Accompanying the relatable resources for her is the book *How to Talk Confidently with Your Child about Sex,* just for you. I found these tools invaluable as I sought to engage my daughter in healthy conversations about sex and God's plan for it.

I'll never forget a night during Courtney's middle school years when she asked me to read aloud to her as she styled my hair. The text was about maturing physically according to God's design, and it talked about what a maturing girl can expect when her menstrual cycle begins. Our conversation that followed was priceless. This resource helped open the door for more detailed discussions about the physical changes she could expect, along with the emotional growth and topsy-turvy feelings that would accompany that growth. Books like these really impacted Courtney in meaningful and applicable ways. From her elementary school years, through the preteen and teen years, and even into early adulthood, I was careful to recommend only those books that spoke from a Christian worldview to address the topics of crushes, dating, modesty, purity, and more.

INAPPROPRIATE TOUCH

Have intentional talks about inappropriate touch, the kind that stands in sharp contrast to positive physical touch. Address the private portions of her body that should never be touched, even by someone she knows and thinks she can trust. You cannot overstate this message for her protection. She needs to know that if someone approaches or touches her in any way that makes her feel uncomfortable, his or her touch is inappropriate. Even if that person tells her it's okay, and especially if they threaten her in any way, she should leave the situation, ignore the threats, and come straight home. That person is wrong and not to be trusted. Teach her to look for red flags and to flee from situations that could put her in harm's way. Recognize and protect her in situations where you may be present. (More than once, I came between my daughter and adults who wanted to touch her when I could tell that their attempts, however innocently intended, were making her feel uncomfortable.)

TEASING
While your precious princess is still very young, inappropriate teasing about boys is going to take place among her peers, in and out of the classroom and in other social situations. This teasing may make her feel uncomfortable, especially when she's years away from adolescence and thinks that boys are still gross—when she doesn't yet understand the concept of having a boyfriend. While you cannot place yourself in the middle of every situation, you can forewarn your daughter about teasing. There will be moments when you can protect her or use a situation for her good.

Such a situation arose in our home when our daughter was blowing out the cake candles on her seventh birthday. Our guests began teasing her, telling her that she had a boyfriend for every candle that she missed. She ran from the room in tears and threw herself on her bed, embarrassed and uncomfortable with their words. I sat beside her and stroked her hair, comforting her and validating her feelings and her reaction, letting her know that the guests were the ones who should feel embarrassed by their inappropriate comments. Perhaps scenarios like these seem harmless enough, but such situations can lead a young girl prematurely into thoughts about the opposite sex that she's not physically or emotionally ready to handle. They can lead her to feel uncomfortable around boys, stifling healthy and normal boy-girl camaraderie that naturally exists in the early elementary years.

PURITY FOR HER PRINCE

Share with your princess your prayer and your desire that she remain sexually pure until she is married. Regardless of what society, secular educational resources, the media, or even her friends are saying, you do not have to adopt the expectation that she will engage in sexual activity before marriage. Despite society's attitude, God's Word is clear: **"Let marriage be held in honor among all, and let the marriage bed be undefiled, for God will judge the sexually immoral and adulterous"** (Hebrews 13:4). Don't be afraid to go against the grain; challenge society's stance, and stand up for the truth. Talk about how precious her purity is from the first time you engage in conversation with her about sex. Take her to God's Word, and teach her the beautiful truth that her body is a temple of the Holy Spirit (see verses below). She is so precious to His Majesty, her Creator, that she was bought at a price—the price of her Savior's blood—for the forgiveness of her sins. God's perfect plan that she remains pure for her prince is also and absolutely for her good. God declares that sex outside of marriage is a sin, and fleeing from that sin is the most self-respecting thing she can do as she glorifies God in her body: **"Flee from sexual immorality. Every other sin a person commits is outside the body, but the sexually immoral person sins against his own body. Or do you not know that your body is a temple of the Holy Spirit within you, whom you have from God? You are not your own, for you were bought with a price. So glorify God in your body"** (1 Corinthians 6:18–20).

Trust that your daughter is part of a generation that would like to be abstinent but desperately needs courageous role models and trusted authority figures to be a voice for them, challenging them to do the thing that may be more difficult and is decidedly countercultural. You can be that voice. She hears you when you talk about sex and marriage. You and your husband are the single most powerful influence on your princess's decisions regarding these matters. (Yes, your influence trumps that of her peers, social media, celebrities, and the like!) According to a 2015 New York Times article, a study conducted by the National Campaign to Prevent Teen Pregnancy polled one thousand teens; according to the survey's results, parents are the largest influence on their children's decisions about sex but often don't realize it While the world intentionally markets sex and a promiscuous lifestyle, you can just as intentionally talk to your teen about abstinence and God's plan for sex. Equip her with the facts, and provide her with your unconditional love and support. Encourage and embolden her to stand strong against the sexual temptations that WILL come her way.

BEFORE SHE BEGINS TO DATE

When your daughter reaches the age where the boys who were formerly gross have suddenly become cool, she may begin to daydream about her future Prince Charming. When your daughter has her first crush, you can let her know that, while the object of her crush may not be her future prince, it's normal for those types of feelings to continue as her physical and emotional growth continue. Talk about those feelings, and nurture her through this time of daydreams. She will likely read fairy tales and see them acted out on the big screen, she may attend weddings, and she'll hear hap-pily-ever-after true tales of others' love and marriage. And she'll dream. She'll dream of one who will find her, romance her, and sweep her off her feet. But long before her dreams become a reality, you have the unique opportunity to gently guide her.

What priorities can you lead her to consider, as a part of your discussions about purity, dating, and sex, even before she enters her potential dating years? First and foremost, instill in her the importance of connecting with a fellow Christian, with whom she would be "yoked" or joined if she were to marry him. As in every other matter, share God's Word concerning this: **"Do not be unequally yoked with unbelievers. For what partnership has righteousness with lawlessness? Or what fellowship has light with darkness? What accord has Christ with Belial? Or what portion does a believer share with an unbeliever?"** (2 Corinthians 6:14–15).

A second priority you can share with your princess, should she decide to date, is setting boundaries and creating a plan for her own protection and for that of the young man of her affections. As you teach her about boundaries, you can pose important questions: Does she know if he shares her morals and values? Does he have the same commitment to sexual purity that she does? Recently, Courtney shared these thoughts with me: "It's all fine and good to say that you're going to remain pure until marriage, but another thing to live it out. You have to have a plan. You should have a boundary set as a safeguard, but 'How far is too far?' is the wrong question. If he doesn't respect the boundary you've set, he isn't worth it and he needs to leave. The ideal guy has his own boundaries too. He wouldn't consider pushing past yours. The right question is 'How can I love this person the most in a Christlike way?' Once both of you decide your boundaries, envision them on a scale; move them up one level, so you're not even touching the boundary. The focus, as you set boundaries in dating, is really on your relationship with Christ. You can set up boundaries, but if your motivation is not centered on the love of Jesus and the desire to do His will, then it will be so easy to stumble." Encourage your daughter to seek His will and His strength.

Third, teach her how to act like a lady, a princess of the King who is worthy of every prince's respect—especially that of the prince she may date. By God's grace, you can model to her what it looks like to be a woman of virtue. How can you witness this within your own walk? As always, look to God's Word and seek His discernment. Ask for self-control as you consider every TV show, movie, YouTube video, or other Internet site you and your growing girl may view. Pray this psalm over her and with her: **"Turn my eyes from looking at worthless things; and give me life in Your ways"** (Psalm 119:37). As shared more broadly in other chapters, consider the modesty of your dress and the demeanor and topics of your conversations with other adults and teens, especially as sex-related topics arise (and they will). How can your words and actions honor God's plan for sex? How can you uphold sexual purity and your commitment to it as a mother of influence, whether you are married, widowed, or divorced?

If you are a single mom, be aware that your daughter will be watching very closely how you interact with men. Sex outside of marriage is a sin, no matter a person's age and regardless of previous relationships. Even if your past example in this area is not ideal, you can use it to explain why God's plan is the best plan and you can use it to teach about repentance. Reassure your daughter that God extends His grace and forgiveness to every sinner, no matter the circumstances.

KISSING FROGS

Do you recall this fun fairy-tale storyline? The princess kisses just the right frog and—poof—it instantly transforms into a handsome young prince who sweeps her off her feet. No girl would kiss a real frog and expect it to turn into a charming prince who is her soul mate. But romantic notions of magical relationships prevail. Fairy-tale romance is perpetuated in movies and on television, in songs and on the Internet. When your daughter reaches an age when she is ready for a boy-girl relationship, you can continue to affirm her dignity and her identity as a godly girl.

★ But what if the popular crowd says that if a girl dresses provocatively, the right guys will suddenly wake up and notice her beauty? Only after she lowers her standards for dressing modestly does she see that the attention she attracted was not the kind she sought.

★ Or what if the cutest guy in class says all the right things and his attention causes her to feel smart and likeable? Only after she falls for him does she find out that he has been filling her with empty flattery just to help him get a good grade and doesn't want anything to do with her outside of class.

★ Or maybe she dates someone with lower moral standards because she's sure that she can transform him into a young man who will love her and treat her like the princess that she is inside. Only after heartbreak does she realize he's still a frog and has no desire to change.

Every growing girl wants to be noticed and accepted, loved and treated like a princess. And in this quest, she may fall for a few frogs, thinking, "If I just do this, wear that, or act a certain way, I can make this person love me. I'll finally feel good about myself."

My daughter recently remarked empathetically, "I've seen girls use sex to feel good about themselves: first because they think it will make them more desirable and second because they think it will protect their relationship. Actually, the opposite is true. If that's the reason he's in the relationship, he may lose interest once he has gotten sex. And third because they think it feels right since they're in love." It's a sad reality that young women who look for validation from others end up feeling worse about themselves, not better, when they realize the prince they sought is still just a frog.

A princess's need to be desired, accepted, and loved will never be fulfilled by a frog, and while these needs may someday be fulfilled by the prince she marries, they can only be *fully* found and fulfilled in Christ. Jesus Christ is the only one who knows her every need and never leaves her side. And above all, He loves her unconditionally; He will always treat her as the princess that she is, chosen and adopted by her heavenly Father, His Majesty.

SWEPT OFF HER FEET

Our favorite fairy-tale princes make our hearts beat a little faster because everything they do is so romantic and heroic. They serenade and sing words of love, they behave bravely and perform heroic and selfless deeds, and they find and rescue their true love! What princess wouldn't be swept off her feet by actions like that? Does your daughter dream that her future Prince Charming will be all that and more? Has she placed him on a proverbial pedestal?

Perhaps fairy tales are partly to blame when our daughters find themselves disappointed with reality, when they see that earthly princes don't appear to live up to those make-believe standards. The truth is, your princess will only be able to enjoy a healthy present or future relationship with a handsome young prince when he doesn't dominate her thoughts, actions, or decisions. He should not be the center of her world or placed on a pedestal; Jesus Christ is the only one who deserves to have that place. She is swept off her feet, first and foremost, with the love of Christ. As her heart becomes consumed with Him, He fills her every need in a way that no one person can or was meant to. Her prince can kneel beside her, also putting Christ first in his life, even ahead of his princess.

What is the strongest bond that holds two people together? Love? Yes, but defined how? The world would tell your daughter that the bond of love is based on human emotions or feelings. Warn her about the ways of the world. Feelings are fickle. Emotions can say, "I don't *feel* like I love you today, so I must not. Maybe I never did." But the bond of love is so much deeper than a mere emotion; it's a sacrifice and a commitment, and it finds its center in Christ, who sacrificed His life out of His committed and unconditional love for us. He chooses to love us, even when we aren't so lovable; He forgives us when we've fallen for fickle feelings; and He restores right relationships, bonded together by sacrificial love. A Christ-centered relationship is deeper and more committed than any feel-good fairy-tale romance.

During her high school years, Courtney opened her heart to me, sharing the peace that she had found concerning relationships. A romantic at heart, she told me that, while she would love to have a special young man come into her life, she realized with God's help that she could be content even if one didn't. She prayed that her greatest desire would be for her Lord. She knew that only He could define who she is and only He could know her fully. Only her Savior could fill her every need. She determined that she would wait patiently for His timing and His plan concerning a special relationship with a young man who might enter her life and sweep her off her feet. She prayed that the Lord would give her future spouse the same peace, the same desire for fulfillment that can be found only in Christ.

CREATED FOR EACH OTHER BY GOD'S DESIGN

As you take your daughter to the Word, teaching her the truth of God's design for sex and marriage, start at the beginning. From the beginning, God created woman to complete man and man to complete woman. **"Then the LORD God said, 'It is not good that the man should be alone; I will make him a helper fit for him'"** (Genesis 2:18). Adam and Eve were literally made—"fit"—for each other; Eve was formed *for* Adam and *from* his very rib. God created male and female to complete each other physically, emotionally, and spiritually.

God designed us for marriage, a divine union that we cannot humanly fully understand, but as in all things, we take God at His Word when He says that, in marriage, the two will become one: **"Therefore a man shall leave his father and his mother and hold fast to his wife, and they shall become one flesh"** (Genesis 2:24). Man and woman physically become one as God designed sex for His beautiful, creative purpose. While He is Creator of all, He chooses this amazing means through which to bring forth the next generation of His creation. He gave us the desire for each other in the love that is meant uniquely and only for man and wife.

Share with your daughter a profound yet basic truth that can be seen in the human anatomy. Every bodily system (circulatory, respiratory, digestive, etc.) is complete and functions independently, with the exception of one. The reproductive system, by itself, whether male or female, cannot function (reproduce) naturally without the other. Alone, it is incomplete. You may use this obvious illustration to make clear to your daughter what the secular world misses: God could have chosen a different means for the creation of future generations, but He chose the beautiful and intimate union of male and female, who together become one flesh in marriage, to create new life.

Jesus held up marriage, restating the words of Genesis and providing the very definition of marriage. As the Pharisees were testing Him and asking what was lawful concerning divorce, Jesus replied, **"Have you not read that He who created them from the beginning made them male and female, and said, 'Therefore a man shall leave his father and his mother and hold fast to his wife, and the two shall become one flesh'? So they are no longer two but one flesh. What therefore God has joined together, let not man separate"** (Matthew 19:4–6). Notice Jesus' further definition of "one flesh" between a man and a woman when He says God has joined them together. It's a spiritual union as well as a physical one.

Adam and Eve's marriage and their love for each other was perfect before they messed it up (see Genesis 3). Because of their fall into sin, their perfect union was blemished. However, they remained united, as husband and wife. Because we are sinners, my husband and I will not be able to have a perfect marriage. Our daughter doesn't look at her parents thinking she'll see Cinderella and Prince Charming. But thanks to God's amazing grace in Christ, our sins are covered with His perfection. **"God abides in us and His love is perfected in us,"** enabling us to **"love one another"** (1 John 4:12) and forgive one another. We can't live up to fairy-tale standards, but we trust that our love story, as part of our life story, is in the author's hands. We protect it and we cherish it; we pray for it and we lay it before the Lord. We look at each other as Christ does: with love and forgiveness.

Your marriage can point the way to a healthy future for your daughter and her prince, if one should come riding into the future pages of her life story. How can you best impact her by your example now? Stand by your husband throughout every chapter of your shared life story. Show him genuine and unconditional love and respect. Your demonstrated care of your husband will speak volumes to her, as she is subconsciously training toward the treatment of her own. Give your husband encouragement and opportunity to build healthy communication and a positive father-daughter relationship with her from the first pages of her life story.

DON'T CONFORM—BE TRANSFORMED!

Our world, at the hands of the evil one, works tirelessly to convince us that sex outside of marriage is not only permissible, but also natural, normal, and even commendable. And it's easy for us and our daughters to fall for these lies and get caught up in emotions because something feels good, especially since the world says so. But that doesn't make it good or right, especially when it goes against God's Word.

My daughter observed, "Girls have set low standards for themselves [regarding sex] because the culture is pushing at them to conform. Girls have been conditioned to think and feel that high standards aren't attainable or necessary." Teach your daughter that feelings, like the world's messages, so often betray us. But she can trust the truth of God's design for sex, a gift to be shared only within the bond of marriage, the bond that exists only between a husband and wife, the two-made-one flesh.

Our contemporary culture would also have us redefine marriage according to whatever people would like it to be and according to their feelings or secular culture's latest ideas regarding sex and marital union. Pause to consider who created and defined marriage in the first place: God. The Creator of marriage—the author of our life stories and the Lord of the universe—designed and defined marriage, and He has stated His unchanging definition of it clearly across Scripture. As you teach this truth to your daughter, remind her also that marriage is not merely a piece of paper, a contract that can be easily ripped in two. It's also not merely the contractual union of any two or more people who want the freedom to love anyone they desire in the unique way that God ordained for the sole union between one man and one woman.

Take a look at the following two verses, noting the first, which directly precedes and leads to God's instructions against conforming to this world: **"I appeal to you therefore, brothers, by the mercies of God, to present your bodies as a living sacrifice, holy and acceptable to God, which is your spiritual worship. Do not be conformed to this world, but be transformed by the renewal of your mind, that by testing you may discern what is the will of God, what is good**

and acceptable and perfect" (Romans 12:1–2). Covered in Christ's perfection, we are made holy and acceptable to God! By His grace and mercy and according to His will, we present ourselves to the Lord for His service. Our lives are not our own (see again 1 Corinthians 6:19); they're not to be lived in conformity to the world but are to be set apart from this world and its ways. By the Holy Spirit's power and through the study of the Word, we can discern God's perfect will regarding sex and marriage, created by His design.

A WORD OF GRACE

Maybe you didn't set a good example in matters of purity during your own growing-up years or even as an adult, and you feel like a hypocrite as you attempt to guide your own daughter down a God-pleasing road in regard to her future or current relationships and as you teach her about God's plan for sex and marriage. Satan would love to trip you up and make you feel unworthy to teach or model purity to your precious princess. The truth is, on our own, we have all fallen short of the life of sexual purity God desires for us. Even if we have abstained from sex outside of marriage, we've thought impure thoughts, viewed sexually explicit TV shows or movies, listened to lyrics that glorify extramarital sex, or something similar. By the Holy Spirit's leading, we come to our Savior with repentant hearts, confessing our impurity to Him and receiving in return His full and free forgiveness, purchased for us by His blood at the cross. We are covered by the purity of Christ and emboldened in Him to live upright and godly lives and to teach our growing girls about God's design for marriage.

During your daughter's growing-up years, she may share

stories of friends who have faced difficult consequences, such as depression, disease, loss of reputation, pregnancy, or even abortion, as a result of a decision to have premarital sex. As she shares, don't be quick to react or judge; instead, offer guidance and grace. As you listen, you may be able to lead her to see for herself the reality of the negative consequences of going outside God's plan for sex. While decisions regarding sex may seem like something to be made in the moment without lasting impact, the consequences can last a lifetime.

Even as we share God's Word and lovingly teach our daughters His plan regarding sexuality, they may fall into sexual temptation, cave to the pressures around them, and find themselves in situations that they regret. What are you to do when your daughter's actions have fallen short of your desires for her? Reassure her of her Savior's love and your love. Continue to communicate openly and honestly with her, and let her know that you are there for her, to walk beside her through heartbreak or trials. She might face life-changing consequences as a result of her decisions, but even in these circumstances, by God's grace, she has the opportunity to live out her faith and uphold life.

None of your sins or hers is beyond the reaches of God's grace in Christ. Lead your daughter to the cross, and remind her of the full and free forgiveness that she receives there, just as you do. She is covered by the purity of Christ; renewed in Him, she is empowered by the Spirit to begin with a clean slate, committing once again to a life of sexual purity, living her life as a testimony to God's grace, and even setting an example for her Christian peers. **"Let no one despise you for your youth, but set the believers an example in speech, in conduct, in love, in faith, in purity"** (1 Timothy 4:12).

SHOW AND TELL

1. Are you nervous or worried about the conversations that you're preparing to share with your daughter? Seek God's strength, search His Word, and solicit the support of others as you rely also on trusted Christian media and resources for help. May God give you excitement to share the beauty of God's design for sex within the uniquely created relationship called marriage.

2. Consider finding or creating a purity covenant. Plan a special *Daughter Date* where you and your husband can present your early-adolescent princess with a covenant, along with a purity ring, if desired. Following are words similar to those contained in the covenant we shared with our daughter as we also presented her with a ring:

FOR WEDLOCK ONLY

Lord, realizing that my body is Yours and that You live in me, I ask You this day for Your help, that I may remain sexually pure until marriage. I promise to keep this covenant and ask for Your strength to resist any temptation to break it. I ask that You also keep my husband-to-be in Your care, strengthened against similar temptations. In Your perfect time, bring us together according to Your will. Lord, You always keep Your promises; help me to keep mine. Remind me of Your love and grace that are mine by faith in Jesus.

Do you not know that your body is a temple of the Holy Spirit within you, whom you have from God? You are not your own, for you were bought with a price. So glorify God in your body" (1 Corinthians 6:19–20).

Dated this _____ day of _____

_____Signature

_____ Witness

3. While you pray for God's will concerning your princess's
    future or current relationships, you can pray for a godly
    young man who will one day sweep your daughter off
    her feet, love her, and complete her (and she, him) in
    marriage. As you do, pray that she would know first
    and foremost that Christ, her heavenly Prince of Peace,
    makes her complete and that He loved her first; He is
    the center of her very existence. Pray for *and* with her,
    asking that the love of Christ would fill and captivate her
    so completely that every young man she meets would see
    that Jesus holds first place in her heart. And pray similar-
    ly for the special young prince who will one day hold her
    heart as well.

4. Share the following words of one teenage girl with your
    daughter, and discuss: "It's easier to choose to remain
    pure when considering your future husband and want-
    ing to save that gift for him. Are you respecting your
    boyfriend's future wife if he doesn't turn out to be 'the
    one'? Are you putting him and his future first? Love is
    about sacrifice, which includes being considerate of him
    and his needs first. Your relationship should be others-fo-
    cused and Christ-centered." Discuss the gift mentioned
    above and what it means for her to give the gift of purity
    to her future husband. Together, consider the significance
    of being others-focused and Christ-centered in regard to
    every relationship.

Chapter 11

The Power of Influence—
Shaping a Princess's Character

Train up a child in the way he should go; even when he is old he will not depart from it. Proverbs 22:6

A LASTING INFLUENCE

*F*amily members were filming a series of live and candid video messages during the grandparents' wedding anniversary celebration, and friends and relatives were sharing humorous memories as they left personal messages throughout the day. When a sixteen-year-old granddaughter took her turn to leave a few words, everyone assumed that she would tell a funny story as many others had, but what she chose to say quieted everyone's laughter and left them speechless. She spoke specifically about her many memories of standing beside her grandpa in church and listening as he sang reverently. She recalled hearing his deep, booming voice and feeling that he was somehow larger than life; she felt safe and loved in his arms. This is how she sees her Lord and Savior. The influence of her grandfather was powerful and lasting. He continually pointed his little granddaughter to Christ and contributed to the shaping of her character from an early age through his reverent example and his loving guidance.

THE POWER OF YOUR INFLUENCE

Many influences, perhaps including that of a godly grandfather, will shape your precious princess's character, powerfully impacting her in every chapter of her life story. Your growing girl is moldable—in the process of being gently shaped into the person the Lord created her to be—and you are blessed with a primary role in that molding process, with God's guidance and strength to back you. As we already established, your level of influence upon her is huge. When you tell her in meaningful and specific ways how valuable and special she is, you'll see her walk with a spring in her step. When you treat her like the treasured daughter of the heavenly Father that she is, you'll see her glow from the inside out, and in response, she'll desire to live up to the title and the character traits that belong to a princess of the King of kings!

You may recall from the introduction that the title "princess" has historically been defined as one who is the daughter of royalty and perhaps even heir to the throne of an earthly kingdom. A princess was known for her character traits, reputed to be reverent, respectful, and obedient. *Your* royal princess is an heir to an incomparably greater kingdom—heaven—by His Majesty's grace through faith in Christ, her fellow heir: **"We are children of God, and if children, then heirs—heirs of God and fellow heirs with Christ"** (Romans 8:16–17).

Your influence upon your impressionable princess touches every aspect of her life, and at the heart of every part is her identity and purpose in Christ. Keeping this truth always before you as you train up your child (Proverbs 22:6) to be reverent, respectful, and obedient, you can model good choices as she sees who and what influences you. You can teach character traits and strengths within the opportunities that are unique to you as you educate her in so many ways and as you equip and prepare her for the future known only by God.

❤ As she grows physically, you can influence her toward good food choices and a healthy lifestyle as you teach her to honor her Creator by caring for the body He designed for her. **"In Him we live and move and have our being"** (Acts 17:28). My daughter recently told me that I probably contributed to her "major sweet tooth," as she calls it, since I crave chocolate constantly. But she also gratefully acknowledged that her father and I tried to be health-conscious for our benefit and for hers, teaching her what constitutes good nutrition, the short- and long-term benefits of eating well, and how poor food choices have a negative impact physically and beyond. While our example has been far from perfect, we've sought to model active lifestyles and have encouraged her to also participate in healthy activities, regular exercise, and fun events.

❤ As she grows socially, you can encourage healthy friendships by modeling your own and by guiding her toward the same, beginning with the positive, Christian influence of your chosen family friends. A mother of three small children shared with me, "We encourage playdates with families who have the same values and morals that we do." One family's genuine and passionate faith in God is quite contagious and can be easily caught by another.

The impact of other royal families upon ours was enormous during our daughter's formative years. Their choices and actions spoke volumes to her, greatly influencing her conduct, her choices of friends, and her actions to this day. **"Even a child makes [her]self known by [her] acts, by whether [her] conduct is pure and upright"** (Proverbs 20:11).

❤ As she grows intellectually, you can teach and model a good work ethic, establishing priority and balance for homework and rest, reading, and other opportunities that will best stimulate her mind for growth. You can be an advocate in her education, partnering with her teachers, who may also have a huge hand in building strong, honest ethics. Teach her to respect earthly authority, beginning at home under the authority of you and your husband. **"Children, obey your parents in the Lord, for this is right"** (Ephesians 6:1). This will serve her well for the rest of her life where all authority is concerned, throughout the season of her education, well into her years in the working world, and ultimately as she recognizes God to be the final and highest authority in all seasons and aspects of life.

❤ Above all, as she grows *spiritually*, you can raise her to revere the Lord and worship Him. Christ is the cornerstone (Ephesians 2:20), the foundation, the very author and founder of your daughter's faith (Hebrews 12:2). Building upon the rock of Christ (1 Corinthians 10:4) as a family, you give her the grounding beneath her feet so that she may stand strong, by the power of the Holy Spirit, as you walk in faith together and impart your influence upon her. Through you, Mom, the heavenly

Father imparts His wisdom as He guides you continually to His Word of truth and as you pass it on to her. If you are passionate about your relationship with Christ, there's a good chance she will be too!

PEOPLE OF INFLUENCE–HER CAST OF CHARACTERS

Consider the cast of characters—past, present, and future—in your princess's life story. What are their roles in her life, and in what ways have they or will they potentially influence her? If she's still very young, her cast may be small, but you can expect it to grow greatly as you anticipate areas where influence will be strong. If she's old enough, ask your daughter to join you as you make a list and then consider each person's impact. Her cast of characters includes you, of course, and her father; it may also include siblings, grandparents, and other extended family. Her list will expand to include her friends, confidantes, and classmates; the persons of authority over her, including teachers, spiritual leaders, and coaches; and even those she may consider her nemeses from time to time.

Together, take a good look at her list. Impress upon her that the people with whom she chooses to spend time are the same people who will have the greatest opportunity to influence her worldview, her beliefs, her character, and her outlook throughout her life story. They will impact the way she speaks and acts, the things she likes, her values and her mindset, and the perception she has of herself.

You have the opportunity to bring people of positive influence into her life. Surround yourself and your family with other faithful Kingdom workers who will also keep watch over your princess. God will use many Spirit-filled people (daycare providers, Sunday School teachers, pastors, youth leaders, and Christian mentors) to influence her and impart His truth through their words and witness.

Teach and mentor your daughter to seek in her closest friends those who would give and receive encouragement and with whom she can be transparent and genuine, without concern for appearances. Guide her toward friends of influence who will hold her accountable and vice versa. And finally, help her seek out friends who share her Christian faith, that they can encourage one another in their faith walks and find joy and passion in similar interests and pursuits.

THINGS OF INFLUENCE

What things of this world influence her? Begin another list that may include such things as music, books, and all kinds of other media, her areas of interest and involvement, that may open doors of opportunity.

Music can wield a powerful and unique form of influence. Lyrics, when combined with a melody, are more easily memorized than words alone and, when played repeatedly, may be retained for a lifetime. Prayerfully consider this when leading her toward music genres in her early years and beyond. Courtney puts it this way: "A message tied to music impacts a person psychologically when the two are combined. The message in much of the music that I listened to while growing up reminded me of the hope I have in Christ. It gave me insight into the heart of God and has shaped who I want to be." She credits the influence of family friends, who introduced her to Christian music from an early age via recorded music and live concerts in addition to hymns and songs of praise in worship. Since then, she's been bombarded by secular music, especially as her social influences have expanded and technology has enabled her to have instant access to virtually any song. While some lyrics available to her are positive, some encourage and promote immoral behavior, disrespect, and violence. As a young adult, she must be discerning as she guards her heart and her mind from mixed and even harmful messages. As her mother, I still pray for that discernment and for her protection.

The words of a good ***book*** can leave a lasting impact on an impressionable girl. Take an avid interest in your daughter's choices in reading. Lead her to the library and to the Christian bookstore. Engage her in picture and chapter books, fiction and non-fiction, that uphold your beliefs and value systems. She may also dive into a wealth of secular titles. Whenever possible, read them yourself and discuss them together: Is the topic or plotline God-pleasing? Can she find allegory or a moral lesson through it? What can she learn about an author's worldview? Consult trusted friends for advice, pray for and with your daughter, and consider when you may need to steer her away from certain titles along with a clear explanation. I'm grateful for the many authors who have influenced my daughter through their books, especially within the genres of Christian fiction and non-fiction; they speak to preteen and teen girls about such topics as purity, modesty, dating, modern idolatry, friends, and life as a Christian girl in today's world.

The influence of ***media*** upon your growing girl is larger today than it's ever been—and growing faster than you can say "cyberspace"! Circle back to chapter 7, *Making Appearances*, for encouragement, advice, and warnings regarding the me-ga-influence of social media in particular, as it may bombard your daughter via smartphone, tablet, or other technological tool that brings the world to her fingertips, eyes, and ears. As in other areas of influence, pray for discernment and protection. And speak freely to her about the benefits and the dangers that exist any time she plugs in to the cyber world. Warn her about predators, bullies, spammers, and scammers, who seek to harm, distract, and destroy. Establish rules regarding TV shows and movies, and explain the choices that you've made for her protection.

Your daughter's *special interests*, as she explores and discovers her gifts in athletics, the arts, and more, can leave quite an impression upon her as she grows. **Church involvement** will have a huge influence on her as she actively serves, volunteers, participates, and grows spiritually through children's, family, and youth ministries. Courtney remembers her experience: "Being involved in church helped shape who I am. It incorporated faith into my everyday life. It wasn't just a Sunday morning thing, but so much more. It connected me with people who believed what I did. Church became a place that was both comfortable and exciting. My best friends, to this day, are those connected to church in some way." Opportunities for your daughter's involvement expand outside the church doors and into the community through service and outreach; they may even expand across the globe through missions. Although the primary purpose of these opportunities is to benefit others and bring the Good News of Christ to them, a boomerang benefit comes to those whose lives are impacted and changed as a result of their service.

PROTECTION AND PREPARATION

When my royalty were still babes-in-arms, I received wise counsel from another mommy. She gently informed me of something that I had difficulty hearing: our mommy vocation is primarily to prepare our little ones to leave the nest and soar successfully. "What?!" I thought. "They're still in diapers!" I knew our role in raising royalty meant that my husband and I were to protect them and provide for them. But prepare them? **"Train up a child in the way he should go; even when he is old he will not depart from it"** (Proverbs 22:6). Before I knew it, my babies would outgrow my arms. Now, all of a sudden, they're almost grown up. I pray this proverb, that they will not depart from the training—the protection and the preparation—that we have provided.

A wise friend counseled me, "Deb, you can protect them to a point, but at some point, society intrudes." It will find its way into your daughter's day in places and situations beyond your control, your home, and even your knowledge. Prepare her, as I shared above, concerning music, media, and more, with intentional prayer and talk time that includes warnings, instruction, and words of discernment so she can stand strong when society intrudes.

Prayerfully consider how you can best protect and prepare her at each age and on each page of these early chapters of her life story. For example, before allowing her to spend the night with a friend, meet with the mother, get to know the family and their specific situation, and establish boundaries and safeguards. Let your daughter know she can contact you at any time. And instill in her trust that will allow her to tell you anything, especially those things that appear to her as a red flag in her interactions with others.

Prepare her by helping her learn to plan for each situation, as much as possible, before she finds herself in the midst of it. If she is joining friends, what are they planning to do together? How can she be prepared to address the situation or make her way out of the situation if her peers begin to use bad language, watch a movie with a rating that goes against your family's rules, or behave inappropriately in any number of ways? Let her know that it's okay to use you, Mom, as the bad guy, if necessary: "My mom said I can't." Courtney and her twin brother came up with comical code names for my husband and me, for use in the event of an emergency, should they need to contact us to get out of an uncomfortable situation without making it obvious or potentially causing them harm. My code name was Crouton. (Silly, I know!) If either child called or texted using this word, I knew to come to the rescue—or at least say "no" on their behalf and for their protection.

As you protect and prepare—as you slowly release your grip upon your beloved princess—remember that even when she is not in your immediate care, you can be confident that she's in the Lord's continual care. She is covered with His protection; He is her safe place—her refuge: **"In the fear of the Lord one has strong confidence, and [her] children will have a refuge"** (Proverbs 14:26).

HER INFLUENCE UPON OTHERS– GUIDED BY GOD'S WORD

Your daughter is a character in others' life stories too, of course. As you talk about influence, ask her to consider the kind of influence she can have on others. Will she be a part of their stories' climax or conflict? In other words, is she going to build up or tear down her cast of characters? As you pray for her and with her concerning the importance of influence, guide her to God's Word, which is the single greatest influence upon her, by the power of the Holy Spirit, who works on her heart, attitude, thoughts, and motives. The Lord provides clear instructions across His Word for living out her story in connection with her fellow characters, that she may be a light to the darkened and lost world around her, a child of God living in the midst of a **"crooked and twisted generation,"** among whom she shines as a light in the world (see Philippians 2:15). The following passage from Romans includes a sampling of these instructions. As you read them, consider the Lord's transforming work in her life as she lives it out according to His Word, as she develops character traits, and as she influences those around her as a result:

> **"Rejoice with those who rejoice, weep with those who weep. Live in harmony with one another. Do not be haughty, but associate with the lowly. Never be wise in your own sight. Repay no one evil for evil, but give thought to do what is honorable in the sight of all. If possible, so far as it depends on you, live peaceably with all."** (Romans 12:15–18)

As she attempts to live harmoniously and peaceably with others, she will quickly learn that it isn't always easy. Fellow classmates and those competing for attention or position may appear, at least for a time, on your daughter's "nemesis" list. Although it may be difficult for her to do so, with the Lord's help, she can treat all people with honor and respect, repaying evil with good, even when those people are behaving dishonorably or disrespectfully. She can live humbly and not haughtily, giving thought to others' needs ahead of her own. She can rejoice and weep with those who need a friend in good times and in bad. Teach her to see that every Christian is an adopted son or daughter of the heavenly Father by faith in Christ, which means they are fellow princes and princesses of the King of kings, even when they're not behaving like royalty. And every person without faith is another person she may introduce to His Majesty, her heavenly Father, and to His Son, the Prince of Peace.

WHEN OTHERS' INFLUENCES LEAD HER TO DOUBT

Cultivate open lines of communication with your dear daughter, which may significantly impact her future ability and freedom to come to you, especially regarding conversations about faith and honest discussions about doubts, fears, and concerns. This is particularly important as she also begins to hear from teachers and peers who do not share her faith. You can reassure her that questions and doubts are normal. Doubt is far from disbelief. In fact, God may use this time of questioning to draw her closer to Himself. So don't panic if your growing girl comes to you expressing doubt about God, the Bible, or her faith. It is vital that she knows she has your unconditional love; then, she'll be much more receptive to ongoing dialogue and to your replies, gentle guidance, and involvement in her life during a time of doubt or questioning.

Any time Courtney questioned details about faith, my initial response included a small inner panic. I could feel my heartbeat in my throat, and I would immediately begin to tremble. My thoughts would race: *Where did this come from? What led her to question this?* I would be tempted to blurt a reply. To react rashly. But when I did, it was rarely received well and just came across as correcting or critical. Maybe my retort made sense, and maybe it was even biblical and entirely true. But if it flew out defensively, it revealed my failure to really listen and respond thoughtfully and carefully. Such a quick, thoughtless response isn't effective and could cause communication to come to a screeching halt. So I learned, instead, to listen.

As your daughter talks and you listen, also silently talk to God, asking for discernment and wisdom in your response. Those times when my heart thumped and my hands trembled, I silently took it to the Lord, simply praying, *Help, God. Help me to really listen. And open my mouth with words that will only help and not hurt.* Know as well that there may be times when you need to say some tough words in response to her doubt and skepticism, especially if her words have come across with apparent disrespect and irreverence toward God. Pray boldly for the ability to speak the truth in love, trusting that God is working for her good and yours. She is likely just feeling confused, even conflicted. Gently work at getting to the bottom of her questions. Why does she doubt? Where are her influences? Knowing her personality, would it be helpful to get her to see that the company she keeps could be damaging to her? **"Do not be deceived: 'Bad company ruins good morals'"** (1 Corinthians 15:33). Or will that only drive her closer to the bad influence? Pray for discernment in addressing this too. And then, take a careful look at your home and family life as you practice your faith. Has your influence been consistent? As we talked about in chapter 6, *Like Mother, Like Daughter*, more is caught than taught. Do your actions match your words? Maybe she misunderstood something you said or did, and it's tearing at her internally. In response, she has begun to doubt. Be real. Confess. Talk to her about it. Go to God's Word.

Trust that God can and will use this time for your daughter to personalize her own faith and to respond to the Holy Spirit's work in her life as she recognizes that her faith is her own and not merely that of her parents. And even if she is questioning you at every turn, don't give up! As powerful as other influences are on her faith walk, those influences will come and go, both the good and the bad. Even the peers who cause her to question, the song lyrics that fly in the face of the Christian faith, and the teachers who claim a competing worldview as truth cannot hold a candle to your influence, Mom. That's right—theirs cannot compare with yours. Your impact can outlast and outweigh all others'. Because you raise her to be a godly girl, to fully rely on God's Word, she'll grow to maturity and not be **"tossed to and fro by the waves and carried about by every wind of doctrine, by human cunning, by craftiness in deceitful schemes"** (Ephesians 4:14). It's vital that she is equipped and influenced by you and other members of the Body of Christ in the midst of everyday life, in which she can be all too easily swayed by the negative and worldly influence of those who would seek to harm her. By His work through you and other godly influences, she will **"grow up in every way into Him who is the head, into Christ"** (Ephesians 4:15).

DON'T CONFORM—BE TRANSFORMED!

Your daughter of the King is on a journey, traveling across the pages of her life story, with eternity set before her. That journey, if likened to a fairy-tale setting, will send her through the deep, dark forest of this world. Although the heavenly kingdom is on the horizon, the evil influences lurking in the forest will attempt to lure her eyes from the horizon to the distractions and deceptions beneath her feet and all around her as she journeys through it.

As a result of the godly influences upon her life and by Christ's redeeming and transforming work in her, she will be able to hear the Lord's voice and follow His lead as she tramples through even the darkest of the woods between the present pages and her *happily ever after.* **"And your ears shall hear a word behind you, saying, 'This is the way, walk in it,' when you turn to the right or when you turn to the left"** (Isaiah 30:21).

There will be other voices, of course. Voices of the world, at the hands of the evil one, will call out to her, attempting to influence her in any direction that will lead her away from the one truth. Deceptive voices will twist the truth to justify worldly and sinful pleasures that feel right in the moment, though they defy God's Word. Lying voices will tell her that the Father's house—His heavenly kingdom—is not really on the horizon. Others will admit that it is, but will make the false claim that any path will get her there, even as it means following another's lead and not Christ's. But she will know better. Your princess has heard Jesus say, **"I am the way, and the truth, and the life. No one comes to the Father except through Me"** (John 14:6). She will be able to discern truth from every cleverly packaged lie!

Shiny things on the forest floor of this world—success, wealth, popularity, and fame—will attempt to lure her astray by attracting her attention and distracting her focus. But again, she knows His voice: **"Do not be conformed to this world, but be transformed by the renewal of your mind, that by testing you may discern what is the will of God, what**

is good and acceptable and perfect" (Romans 12:2). She will be able to discern His will as she continues to listen to Him. He will guide her safely through every rough patch as she looks up to Him for help: **"I lift up my eyes to the hills. From where does my help come? My help comes from the LORD, who made heaven and earth"** (Psalm 121:1–2). By God's grace and strength, she'll be able to **"lay aside every weight, and sin which clings so closely, and . . . run with endurance the race that is set before [her], looking to Jesus, the founder and perfecter of [her] faith, who for the joy that was set before Him endured the cross, despising the shame, and is seated at the right hand of the throne of God"** (Hebrews 12:1–2). One day, she will come before the throne and worship her Savior face-to-face!

A WORD OF GRACE

A dear friend and fellow mom talked to me about her two daughters' observable responses to her influence on them. While much of my friend's influence has impacted her daughters positively, she humbly admits that it's often the negative things that are most recognizable to her. She said, "When I see their impatience, their anxiety over a situation, or the critical spirit in which they sometimes address each other, I can feel defeated by the lack of good fruit in them." We can relate, can't we? While we desire to influence our princesses, shaping their character in every good and godly way, sin trips us up, and we fall flat on our faces. We also fail to protect them from other negative influences or point them to people who can make a lasting and positive impression upon them. Praise God for His gift of grace, freely given through faith in Christ.

My friend continued, "I would encourage any mom who hastens to see good fruit in her children to give this concern to Christ each morning when she awakes." Acknowledge your shortcomings, and turn them over to your Lord and Savior. As you seek His forgiveness, ask Him to fill you with the good fruits of love, joy, peace, patience, kindness, and more (see Galatians 5:22–23). These are fruits that will impact your daughter as she witnesses your humble walk with the Lord and as your influence continues to impact her positively, by God's grace, throughout all the ages and stages of her life story in Christ.

SHOW AND TELL

1. Consider the primary areas of influence in your own life in which you can model good choices for your daughter. Who and what influences you physically? socially? intellectually? spiritually? Contemplate one specific action step you can take in each area, with God's help, to intentionally impress a good choice upon your princess.

2. Establish a game plan in which your daughter is equipped to flee from a situation that would compromise her character, though the world says it's okay or even good. Help her to see that there is a way out of every situation-turned-bad, and teach her to look to God's Word for discernment in determining right from wrong in each situation.

3. Keep watch for anything that can try to take your daughter's eyes off the truth. You and your husband are protectors over the palace and over the life of your princess. And while you protect and provide, you also prepare.

❤ Do you have a finger on the pulse of your daughter's life? What are her struggles and fears? How can you come alongside her to let her know you care about everything that influences her?

❤ What is she excited about? How can you steer her interests, from early on, toward God-pleasing, healthy habits, hobbies, and commitments that may impact her positively for years to come?

❤ What's happening in school? Who does she talk about and share time with? How can you impact and gently direct some of her friendships, get to know families of these friends, and even learn to look for red flags?

❤ How does she think media may influence her, for good or for bad? Teach her about desensitization. Discuss the phrase "garbage in—garbage out," and share examples. Ask her to consider specific ways that she can be "in the world but not of the world" with God's help.

4. As God's Word works to transform your princess and develop her character qualities, she is able to influence others for their benefit too. Together, consider the influence she can have as she follows God's instructions for living out her life story in connection with her fellow cast of characters. Read Ephesians 4:25–32 in light of these benefits. (For example, why do honest work? To have something to share with anyone in need. Why speak in a certain manner? That it may build up and give grace to those who hear her.) Look with her through each portion of this passage, and talk about her opportunities to influence others for Christ. Choose other related passages, and sift through them similarly.

Conclusion

Leaving the Palace—
A Princess Prepared for Her Happily Ever After

I have no greater joy than to hear that my children are walking in the truth. 3 John 1:4

PREPARED

*O*ne day, your precious princess will pack her bags and get set to leave the palace. When that day comes, trust that she will be prepared for her happily ever after, even as she continues to grow in faith throughout her life story.

By God's grace and in His strength, you are raising her according to His will. You've brought her to the waters of Baptism, and you share the Scriptures with her, trusting the Holy Spirit's faith-producing and faith-growing work in her through the Word and Sacraments, God's Means of Grace. You're able to instill in her that her true identity is found in

Christ as you lead her to a life in the Word, both in the palace and beyond the palace gates, and as you approach God's throne of grace with your daughter and on her behalf.

With the Lord's help, you're able to reveal to your growing girl the meaning of true beauty, and she'll even seek to imitate your qualities. In God's wisdom, you can guide her through every growing pain as you give her the gift of your presence. By His mercy, you're able to teach her to honor God in her body, created by His design. By your godly influence and that of others, her character traits can be shaped and developed. Every time you look to God's Word for direction, you model discernment, showing her how and where to seek answers, as she grows to make decisions on her own.

God has a plan for your daughter, so remind her, when you help her pack her bags, that He is the author of her faith and the Lord of her life story. His ways are best, and she can trust Him with every turn of the page as her story unfolds, even as she may still look to you, Mom, for grown-up guidance now and then!

THE DAY OF JESUS CHRIST–HAPPILY EVER AFTER

The apostle John said of his spiritual children, those who he nurtured in the faith after bringing them the Gospel: **"I have no greater joy than to hear that my children are walking in the truth"** (3 John 1:4). So we also say of our children, whom God gave us to raise. As you walk in the Gospel truth together across the early pages of her life story, trust each day **"that He who began a good work in [her] will bring it to completion at the day of Jesus Christ"** (Philippians 1:6).

Remember the classic good versus evil storyline mentioned at the beginning of chapter 1? For all who are in Christ, the victory of good defeating evil is a done deal. **"It is finished"** were the final words of Christ at the cross (see John 19:30) as He gave up His life, securing our victory against sin, death, and the evil one when He rose three days later in triumph. Although we will struggle in this world because the evil one still rears his ugly head, we have the power of the Lord on our side, and it's no contest. **"He who is in you is greater than he who is in the world"** (1 John 4:4). Jesus has delivered us from death to life. Eternal life.

You see, this life is akin to the introduction and perhaps the first chapter when compared to the length, depth, and richness of the never-ending life story that is to unfold. Your princess's life in Christ contains the ultimate happy ending. It's not an end at all, but rather a continuation of the eternal life she has in Him. No matter how her story is reading today, her *happily ever after* that God has prepared for her in Christ is far better and more beautiful than you or she can possibly imagine.

Jesus said, **"In My Father's house are many rooms. If it were not so, would I have told you that I go to prepare a place for you? And if I go and prepare a place for you, I will come again and will take you to Myself, that where I am you may be also"** (John 14:2–3). Our Savior and Prince of Peace promised that He will come again. In the day of Jesus Christ, when He returns at the final resurrection, He will raise up your precious princess and all who believe to receive imperishable, glorious bodies: **"But our citizenship is in heaven, and from it we await a Savior, the Lord Jesus Christ, who will transform our lowly body to be like His glorious body"** (Philippians 3:20–21). And He will take her home to Him that she may live forever, a princess of the King of kings, in her heavenly Father's house.